HOW TO BOOST
YOUR PRIVATE INVESTIGATION BUSINESS INTO ORBIT: MAKE $1,000 EVERY WORKING DAY.

John A Hoda
CLI, CFE

How To Boost Your Private Investigation Business Into Orbit: Make $1,000 Every Working Day!

Copyright John A. Hoda (2019)

All rights reserved. No part of this publication may be reproduced, stored in a retrieval system, or transmitted in any form or by any means with the prior written permission of the publisher.

ISBN: 978-0-9890201-6-9

Requests to publish work from this book should be sent to john@johnhoda.com.

Cover and Interior Illustrations, Titling, and Interior Layout: Creative Jay (creativejay.com)

HOW TO
BOOST
YOUR
PRIVATE INVESTIGATION
BUSINESS INTO ORBIT

MAKE $1,000 EVERY WORKING DAY!

John A Hoda
CLI, CFE

INTRODUCTION

JOHN A. HODA

You are a licensed private investigator, and you own an investigations business. You may exceed expenses with your revenues, but you don't have a plan for taking your business to the next level.

Maybe you are tired of treading water with all the exertion needed just to stay afloat.

You might be planning to start your PI business but are unsure how to expand your business once you start making enough money to pay your bills.

For those slogging along or just starting out, we are talking about "boosting" your business.

I use an orbiting rocket for this book in the series. Overcoming gravity and the drag of the atmosphere is paramount for a successful launch, but the rocket scientists figured out they need a booster stage to take the payload into a sustainable orbit where only a tiny amount guidance and thruster energy, by comparison, is needed to give you those beautiful photos from space. I thought long and hard on this analogy both for internal resistance (gravity) and external forces on your business (atmospheric

INTRODUCTION

drag) and how to overcome them with a booster rocket (Ideas from this book).

The concept of making $1,000 every working day is the orbiting goal. How does $261,000 a year sound? The experts say 261 days is the average number of working days a year. That number does not include holidays and vacations. Let's assume you take all the holidays and two weeks of vacation. You would still be looking at around 240 days a year or $240,000. That is a lot of money for most people, but it also sounds a little daunting and may be unachievable. I am told that you eat an elephant one bite at a time. I have never eaten an elephant. It doesn't sound appealing, so let's change the analogy to, "Let's take it one day at a time."

Can you do this as a solo? Yes. Is it better to have some help? Yes. Want to own a business that runs without you in fulfillment or operations? I will give you an example of how that works. For that example, you will need to make more than $261K a year, but we will cross that bridge when we come to it if you choose to work every weekday every week.

Whether you are a solo practitioner or have a team working with you, it is possible to invoice $1,000 a day, every working day. "Whoa," you say, "if that is your top line, what is the bottom line after overhead? What about taxes?"

I agree. We need to define "make" right now.

"Make" means gross - How much you gross each working day.

"Make" is not net. It is not after you take out all your expenses apportioned for that day.

"Make" is not net after taxes. It is not after your expenses and your taxes apportioned for that day.

"Make" is the top line — revenue - even above the cost of goods sold (COGS).

Stop here if you think I misled you. If you are not interested in learning how to receive payments from clients and/or customers to the tune of almost a quarter-million a year, I will gladly refund your money for this book.

If you gross $1,000 a day, but it costs you $1,250 in overhead, then we are not talking about an orbiting rocket, but a sinking ship on its way to the bottom. So, we will be mindful of expenses from here on.

Part of the reason I focus on the top line is simple. You have a daily goal. You have to set up enough cases you can plan to execute $1,000 of invoices every working day. To have enough cases that you bill a grand every working day means you need to have enough cases in your pipeline. To have enough cases in your pipeline, you need a steady flow of clients and/or repeat customers. To have a steady flow of clients and/or repeat customers, you need a scalable and repeatable marketing program. Of course, all this is predicated on you providing a service that meets or exceeds customer expectations which you can deliver efficiently.

You invoice your time either hourly, on flat rates, by contract, or with a budget. Hourly is a simple calculation.

INTRODUCTION

For example, you bill $150 an hour for some work. Your other services have a weighted average. For example, you perform an asset check and charge a flat rate of $350, and it takes you two hours on average.

You make $175 an hour for that flat rate. In this example, we'll say you bill four hours to a file and do one asset check. You invoice $950 for the day. Oh, that was close.

If you can break your goal down to daily billing, it gets a lot simpler to work backwards from there.

I will tell you here. I did not hit a home run with my first business. If I did, that would be boring. I made mistakes, and I stubbornly continued to make those mistakes. It was not until the market changed like quicksand under my feet that I scrambled and learned how to run a business.

Until then, I managed a group of highly-trained employees. I focused on learning more about our tradecraft than the business of investigations. I stumbled and made false steps until I couldn't take my own gravity (resistance) any longer. Even then, I had to take baby steps before I could walk.

It is better to learn from my mistakes than spend time, money, and emotional attachment to chasing down the dream along the wrong path. These lessons were hard-earned, and I hope to point them out to you so you can avoid stepping on snakes when you are lost in the weeds.

If I say to you, "Do as I did to change your attitude and to begin implementing sound business advice," you would only get a narrow view of my path.

Instead, I have created two other characters with different backgrounds, goals, wants, need, and fears. Their companies meet utterly different customer segments. We'll watch them launch and learn how they market to those segments in the two previous books in this series. On this spectrum of investigation company business models, you will find advice to meet your specific needs and get ideas you may never have considered.

Now that they are further down the road, they are making money and doing well, but cannot continue to throw more time and energy at their success. They must grow, or they will slowly stagnate and possibly quit from burn-out.

INTRODUCTION

Meet Tony

Tony Russo lives in Queens with his wife as empty-nesters. As he was getting ready to retire from NYPD as a Detective Sergeant in charge of a squad of detectives in Mid-Town Manhattan, he realized he and his wife were living above their means and had to reign in expenses.

The Russo and Associates start-up was as much about freeing himself from the layers of bureaucracy at the Police Department as tightening their belts to pay off debt. Tony carefully ruminates on what he wanted his business to look like and decides on a Professional-to-Professional (P2P) mode (a term I coined), to provide services to small businesses, Attorneys, and CPAs that deal with businesses with repeat investigative needs.

It is very much a person-to-person approach, and Tony learns to show up regularly at meetings, seminars, conferences, leads groups, and other places where his target audience meets and drinks.

Unexpectedly, he finds he enjoys working in neighboring Nassau County for Criminal Defense attorneys with clients considered to be innocent of the charges. He is wildly successful in his first case, and his face is plastered across the newspaper headlines and on TV in Long Island.

He is busier than he wants to be, and he contemplates a different end to his second career.

Meet Beth

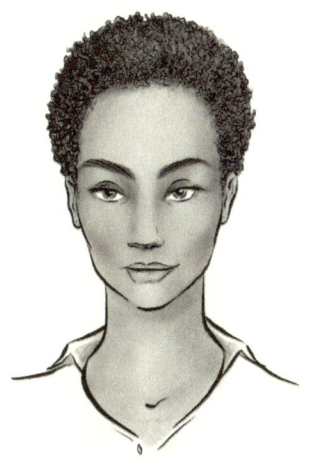

Beth Clark lives and works in Austin, TX. She is a two-tour army veteran who specialized as an Intelligence analyst in Afghanistan. She was working for an armed guard company when she caught the bug to start her own business.

She had the pre-requisite skills and experience to get her PI license and slowly launched her B2C Business-to-Consumer (B2C) company, Truth Be Told Investigations, Inc. with incredible results providing infidelity surveillance and background checks to consumers in the Greater Austin area.

Beth comes into this start-up with no preconceptions. She understands her WHY (the reason she wants to do this work): to provide quality service to regular people who need it, without the layers of bureaucracy she had to endure in the army or guard service.

She builds her business to sell so she can retire early and do adventure travel. She builds her business around Inbound marketing of attracting and keeping prospects on her website until she or her employees can close the deal.

Her outbound marketing of visiting businesses catering to upscale women in the area produces high-margin cases and an equally repeatable and scalable marketing method, which she expands by offering referral commissions to those hair stylists, aerobics instructors, and wellness professionals who point their clients her way.

She is at the cusp of expansion or exhaustion. In her present work, she discovers a real talent and passion for OSINT (open source intelligence) searches.

INTRODUCTION

Her upscale female clients hire the best lawyers in Austin to handle their divorces based upon the , and background checks Beth's company conducts. These high-powered law firms and their growing corporate client base are clamoring for Beth to do extensive Intelligence analysis.

She is at a crossroads where she has to decide between sitting in a sweltering surveillance van, peeing in a coffee can, on a hot, humid summer weekend evening to get video of Mr. Smith and Mrs. Jones committing adultery, or sitting at her desk in an air-conditioned office during regular work hours, churning out reports for grateful, high-paying clients.

Does she grow her B2C business to meet their growing demand?

Does she pivot into B2B and rebrand?

Does she split the baby in half and do both?

Meet John

I talk about my experience in the third person. Where Tony and Beth are modern days, my experience occurred in 2004.

John has just crash landed Independent Special Investigations. ISI was a B2B providing insurance fraud investigations for Property & Casualty Insurance companies in the Northeast.

Armed with a 1986 Oldsmobile, a 386 computer, and a borrowed surveillance camera. He took his Rolodex of contacts and went out on his own Labor Day weekend of 1997.

John is a former police officer, insurance fraud investigator, and claims manager who taught a cadre of hard-working employees in his expertise.

Things were going great. He was growing his staff and territory to meet his goal of being a super regional powerhouse, "From Bangor to Baltimore."

Then a significant disruption in the industry essentially commoditized his services.

He was fond of saying his company were artists and the industry was now hiring house painters. That attitude didn't help him change his mindset until it was too late.

Two national firms, using the latest technological advances (claims adjustors could check the status of their cases online in the earliest of dashboards), went to the highest levels in the claims departments and locked down nationwide two-year contracts.

INTRODUCTION

Local PIs who once had great relationships with their local claims departments and SIU (Special Investigation Units) were now like kids banned from their favorite candy stores. This was a harsh lesson in learning about users as opposed to the ultimate buyers of services.

John became a solo DBA as Squire Investigations after he parted ways with his team. Most were able to parachute to safety, but he had to lay off one employee. It was painful for John and the valued employees. He broke the unspoken agreement of happily ever after.

He began learning about Criminal Defense investigation and Forensic Genealogy. The former was a skill set he had never considered, and the latter was a new Bright Shiny Object.

John had pared down his expenses and, as a solo, was taking home more money than he did with all the overhead from ISI.

He still wasn't making $1,000 every working day and had no plan to do so. His wife was working, and the kids had been out of daycare for a decade. The pressure was not as high as when he first went out on his own.

He was still recovering from the sting of having to start over. He was going to learn from his mistakes but was not sure how to start the rebuilding process.

One thing was for sure: the call to create a company he could sell to employees was as strong as ever. He would learn the right way to grow a company.

JOHN A. HODA

DISCLAIMER

PLEASE READ

I have done my best to give you useful and accurate information in this book, but I cannot guarantee that the information is correct or will be appropriate for your particular situation. Law, procedures, and regulations change frequently and are subject to differing interpretations. It is your responsibility to verify all the information and the laws discussed in this book before relying on them. Noting in this book can substitute for legal advice and cannot be considered as making it unnecessary to obtain such advice. In all situations involving local, state and federal law, especially as it relates to PI regulations and carrying weapons, receive specific information from the appropriate government agency.

OVERVIEW

This book introduces you to well thought-out business decisions (Strategy) and gives you the tools (Tactics) needed to boost your business to the next level.

**Section One:
Stagnate, Change, Grow,
or Slowly Die (Page 17)**
- Strategy
- Tony's story- Changing the ending
- Beth's Story- Pivot and Sell to Competitor
- John's Story- Pivot to B2C and then IMHF

Section Two: Just Do It. Increase Revenue. (Page 39)
- It Depends
- Raise rates
- Fire Customers
- Upsell and Affiliate Marketing

SECTION Three: WEARING fewer HATS (Page 55)
- Jobs You Shed Depend On Your Customer Segmentation
- Tony
- Beth
- John

SECTION Four: Hiring (Page 71)
- Hiring Checklist

SECTION Five: Do As I Say And As I Do (Page 83)
- Training Checklist

SECTION Six: Huddling (Page 93)
- Taking A Page From The Great Game Of Business

SECTION Seven: Sharpening the Saw (Page 103)
- What Got You Here, Won't Get You There
- John: Action Coaching Business Coach
- Tony: Mastermind or Pick Four
- Beth: APPSUMO, Thrive, Hubspot

SECTION Eight: Booster Rocket Engine, Engage! (Page 115)
- Tony
- Beth
- John
- Endings are beginnings
- Conclusion

SECTION ONE:
STAGNATE, CHANGE, GROW, OR SLOWLY DIE

SUCCESS IN THE LONG RUN

I will address a plan for a solo to make $1,000 every working day, but it requires meticulous crafting. I will submit it to you towards the end of the book after you taste all the different recipes. Then if you want to remain a solo, you will have a more full understanding of what that entails as a lifestyle business.

Success has its advantages. You have more work than you can handle. You are not visiting your post office box every morning to see if checks are there. You are not robbing Peter to pay Paul on your bills. Nobody is breathing down your neck or threatening you with collections.

As you grow your business, you could be breathing more relaxed, but you are breathing harder because you have more work in any given day and you still have to administrate it, invoice it, and account for it. These tasks are known as backroom operations.

Not to mention the marketing you need to enact, sooner rather than later.

Many investigators operate under the false impression that when things are going great, they don't have to market anymore. They can just work at what they do best, their investigations (Fulfillment). However, when the pipeline starts to dry up, they take on work they might not usually take on, or they take it on a deep discount just to pay the bills, and before you know it, they are racing to the bottom.

If you know better than to forego marketing, you keep the pipeline full, and now you have to hire help. Working seven days a week, week in and week out gets old. You don't even have time to hire help.

Now here is the fun part. You get so busy that you start making mistakes. You catch so many fish you are in danger of swamping the boat. You are getting the work done, barely, but are delayed on reporting the results.

You put off your regular, steady clients to take on new and promising better-paying work (which doesn't pan out) and now your best clients are no longer calling you, and you don't notice (or care) until your nets are empty.

You may start cutting corners or taking short cuts. For a while, nobody notices, until it blows up in your face.

Your best client sends you back the bill for the time and effort you spent unsuccessfully trying to find their client. Seems their paralegal called 411 (yes, old-fashion directory assistance) and connected with their client.

Are you going to tell the client you failed to note the only time you tried that same number, unearthed from your databases, you got a busy signal? You never tried the number again. You forgot in your haste.

You have to rebuild the trust you worked so hard to earn. You confess your own success is doing you in and you recommit to provide the service you promised. You rip up the bill. You are not happy with the quality of your work. You are better than that.

In desperation, you decide to hire. Your second mistake, it may be worse than the first. Depending on what you hire that person to do, you most likely abandon that job function to them. I pray, for your sake, it does not include handling money or clients directly.

At first, you breathe easier. You might even get your weekends back. You take that vacation your significant other has been bugging you about for months.

Things seem to be working okay. Your new hire (last name, Friday) handles the easy stuff and takes some of the load off your shoulders. You are even thinking about surprising Friday with a raise.

You come back to your office after a significant time away with only minimal email and text contact with Friday, to find they are quitting without notice, and have been sandbagging you and your clients about the work they were doing in your absence.

Friday feels justified because they were never properly trained. They were not told what the expectations were. They were never shown what satisfactory performance looks like.

Friday complains that payroll was always screwed up and you didn't pay them for all the overtime (and you didn't create an HR manual to clear up confusion on the subject).

Friday threatens to call the Department of Labor unless you honor the last pay sheet they submitted. Friday's files reflect less than 20 hours of work, yet you are being extorted for 80 hours of pay. The clients will be screaming - the same clients you almost lost once already.

The calm restorative relaxation from your vacation is now a faint memory as the acid churns in your stomach.

So you meet Friday in a Walmart parking lot half-way between your locations. Friday hands you shaky video and incomplete reports for only a portion of the work on the timesheet. Your

SECTION ONE: STAGNATE, CHANGE, GROW, OR SLOWLY DIE

equipment looks like it was dragged through the mud. Friday repeats the threat, and you reluctantly turn over the final check. You watch Friday burn rubber.

A month later, you get a call from the Department of Labor acting on Friday's overtime complaint.

You vow never to hire another person as long as you live, which is your next mistake and react to the crisis by suspending marketing and turning down new work.

You are now sliding down the slippery slope of your own success. This stagnation is the road to a slow death.

If you planned for growth, your early and hard-won success would not cause the demise of your business.

Instead, what if you plan for your growth instead of acting surprised and unprepared when it happens?

As you watched your numbers grow faster than you planned, you accelerated your hiring plans. Yes, it means more work at a time you can ill-afford it, but at least it is under your control, and you are reacting to the anticipated growth, rather than have the growth soon weigh on your shoulders.

Each evening after dinner, sit down and speed up your work on:

- A recruiting checklist
- A hiring checklist
- An HR protocol for getting employee documents filled out and getting them on the payroll before their start date: hire letters, I-9, W-9s, a real application form with language allowing you to pull credit reports DMV and fingerprint checks. Probationary language in both the application and new hire letter. I liked hiring a person at X pay rate and spelling out that, after 60 days of satisfactory performance,

they would receive X plus 10% as their pay. At the sixty-day mark, they would receive their first evaluation following a process that clearly defined satisfactory performance in their training sessions. We would either part company, or they would receive a bump.

- HR handbook for the little things like Holiday, Vacation, Sick Time, and Overtime. The stuff that keeps you out of trouble with the Department of Labor, if things go sideways with your employees: a boilerplate code of conduct, rules on tardiness, absenteeism, attire, maintenance of and an inventory for equipment, and so on.
- Benefits/Workers Compensation forms/Auto insurance coverages
- Training Plan and Checklist
- Employee evaluation process
- Annual performance reviews

The hiring process shows the applicant you are serious about the importance of their hire to the overall health of the company. The care you take in their selection, the commitment you make to their training, and their supervision pay off huge dividends.

Throwing warm bodies at a problem is a band-aid at best, and it can make the situation worse.

Ask them to fill out a multi-page application. Question it closely. Call the references and the prior employers. Pull the credit report and do the DMV check. Then send them a pre-interview questionnaire. Have them return it before setting up the time and place for the interview.

Once there, take the time to explain the job description, your expectations and show them the training curriculum and performance evaluation.

If the only questions you get are about pay, benefits, vacation time, and sick days, you may have gone deep into the process, but it was better to shake hands and part company.

If, on the other hand, they sound excited about the challenges they will encounter and the growth opportunities presented, you will have 60 days to kick their tires. You can test this vibe out with persons new to the business or persons that have been to the rodeo a few times. The veteran investigator can be enthusiastic about the opportunity to be treated well and will relish the opportunity to show off their skills to someone who will take the time to appreciate them. It also gives you a chance to watch for bad habits ingrained from their previous jobs.

So far, I have concentrated on finding a replacement for you or an addition to you in fulfillment.

What if we talk about your next hire being in operations?

Can the checkbook handle it?

Can you run the numbers to see if you can support it?

Counter-intuitive, you may say, but let's see how Tony, Beth, and John handle the growth.

Tony's Story: Sell

I didn't sign up for this, Tony says to himself. He has been running flat-out for weeks. The growth in his P2P business is steady, then explodes when the Nassau County District Attorney's office drops charges on a murder case Tony worked on. The former DA, now Criminal Defense attorney, Abe Schwartz, who helped Tony get started by introducing him around the Bar Association, told Tony he had an innocent client.

Tony performs an investigation that completely contradicts the State's probable cause for arrest. It forced the State's hand. The publicity results in Tony taking on more and more Criminal Defense cases, some for a premium and some for "Low Bono," as he jokingly refers to not-quite Pro Bono cases.

His carefully laid business and marketing plans didn't account for this growth.

Where he once had time to work his business cases at a crisp pace, the docket calls for Criminal Defense—and spending two to three weeks non-stop during trial—is kicking his ass.

He likes all the work. Correction, he loves the work, especially dissecting and exploiting the weaknesses in the Nassau County cases and finding reasonable doubt.

He didn't take on the NYPD by choice. Tony doesn't want to be staring at detectives from his old precinct days. This is different from managing the flotsam and jetsam of cases back in the Midtown squad room. Here, the system is failing the innocent while

SECTION ONE: STAGNATE, CHANGE, GROW, OR SLOWLY DIE

real criminals are on the street creating mayhem. The victims are not being served by the false arrests either.

He had planned to "keep it small and keep it all." This is supposed to be a second career. For gosh sakes, he already had a pension from his first job. The long hours are both exhilarating and exhausting. This is supposed to be his lifestyle job. He eases off the marketing, and his shadow does not grace the doorway of many of the meetings he once faithfully attended. Tony had planned to work this gig until his wife was ready to retire from her Board of Ed job.

Meanwhile, the Russos benefit from the upsurge in work. They are careful with their expenses after Tony did the math during his launch phase and saw that they were over-extended on credit again. Twice, they had remortgaged their house to consolidate debt.

Pulling the reigns in on their spending, combined with Tony's unplanned growth in revenues have the desired impact on their finances. He is paying off debt, supplementing his 401K, and they refinance the mortgage to a 15-year note. Tony plans to work long enough to guarantee a retirement where they can live well, but not extravagantly. The extra money also allows them an occasional treat. What if he could make more money and leverage his success? Would that speed up the clock to his full retirement? Would that allow him a better retirement plan?

About the time Tony is pondering the predicament of his success, he learns the judge got sick during lunch and didn't return to the bench. The trial is adjourned to the next week giving him some breathing room to reassess.

He had no further to look for an answer than his friend, the former DA. After switching sides of the aisle, Abe started as a solo and now has an office support staff, paralegals and a few hand-picked former DAs and associates fresh out of law school. Their practice mix is a mirror image of Tony's. Is that coincidence?

SUCCESS IN THE LONG RUN

In the following scene, Abe and Tony pack up the exhibits and make the long walk out to their cars in Nassau County courthouse parking lot in Mineola, NY.

"Abe, what have you gotten me into?"

"What do you mean, this is a good case; we are going to win it." Abe retorts.

"Not the case, Abe. All of it. Some days, I don't know whether I'm coming or going."

Abe laughs. "Things could be worse Tony."

"Not that I'm not grateful for all you've done for me, Abe, but I think I may have bitten off more than I can chew. Like this weekend, instead of taking it easy like a retired detective should, I am billing out cases and working on my quarterly reports."

They get to their cars and talk as attorneys, and their investigators sometimes do, but this conversation takes a different tact.

"What's your plan, Tony. How did you see Russo & Associates growing?"

"Honestly Abe," Tony says, playing on the words, "I had planned to turn off the lights and lock the door when we got our retirement nest egg to where we wanted it. I was going to ride off into the sunset with a more secure retirement than if I had just taken my pension."

Abe shakes his head. "You're building value with your brand. It's a shame just to walk away from it. If you could snap your fingers and make it perfect for you, what would you do?"

"I would hire an admin to do my books and open and close the cases. I would hire an investigator to take over most, but not all, of the business cases, and I would train a young gun on how to do the Criminal Defense work. I would cherry pick the cases that are most interesting to me and still be the face of the company for marketing.

SECTION ONE: STAGNATE, CHANGE, GROW, OR SLOWLY DIE

I'd be home most nights and weekends unless it's something hot or we are going to trial." The words flow out in a rush.

"What else?" Abe asks.

"I would eventually turn over the marketing and hire more investigators whom I would manage and occasionally ride along with, so I that don't forget what it's like to be a living, breathing real-life detective."

"And?" Abe prods again.

"I would sell it to them." Boom! There. Tony says it, and everything falls into place.

"Okay, doesn't that sound better than riding off into the sunset?" Abe waves and gets into his car.

Tony sits in his car on a sun-splashed day, admires the fall foliage and writes out the 5-year plan in his notebook. He looks at it and realizes he had a succession plan. Now, all he has to do is put it all together on the fly.

Beth's Story: Pivot / Sell to Competitor

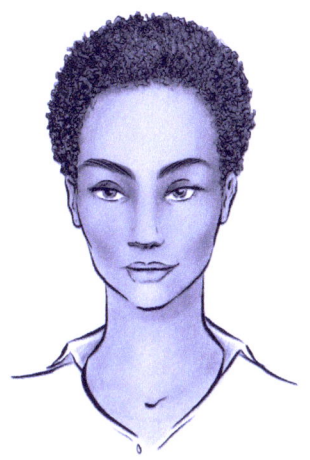

The pie chart on Beth's laptop said it all. First, there was the revenue from the inbound marketing on her website.

When a spouse suspects their betrothed of stepping out, he or she goes online to look for a private investigator. They enter keywords in the search bar of their favorite browser, and Truth Be Told Investigations, Inc. comes up first (after the paid ads). This was no accident.

The person's eye zeroes in on the deliberately worded, A/B tested cache phrases and then click on the link to the website and see testimonial after testimonial before the website fully loaded. The slider below the banner then parades more testimonials across the screen. This website is optimized for all display screens, especially cell phones. Then there are the video testimonials of women talking about choosing Beth Clarke. A live chat pop-up populates the home page with Beth's face and the number. If the person clicks away before they could leave the site, an offer for a free report comes up.

All the viewer has to do is give Beth their email address or phone number for the free report on "The Seven Signs Your Spouse is Cheating on You." That free report rotates with surveillance video of a couple kissing and groping in their car at a secluded part of a well-known park before the email/phone ask pops up.

A six email auto-responder gives the viewer more reasons to know, like, and trust Beth and Truth Be Told over the next several days - always with the pop up for the live chat. Beth and her employees, Mary and Pat, field the phone calls and move the callers through the sales funnel to click on the retainer agreement and add their credit card or Paypal to become a customer.

Using her army training to plan the surveillance like recon missions results in superior results, garnering more testimonials and referrals. Beth prices the surveillances economically with 4, 6, and 8-hour flat rates. No drive time, no mileage. Video is uploaded to a secure, password-protected cloud server.

This slice represents the most extensive time commitment to sell, administrate, and investigate, but it also represents the smallest slice of revenue.

The next slice is twice the size and represents her outbound marketing of upscale women who frequent businesses that cater to them. Beth went to these service-related businesses and made her pitch. She gave free surveillances to some of the workers who had their suspicions that their significant others might be getting something extra on the side.

Even with a cut going to the business people that referred new clients, Beth still makes twice the money on these custom-made longer-tail investigations. She can charge more using multiple investigators per surveillance and other technologies allowed under state law. Because most of the woman are referred, her consultation time yields a higher conversion of prospects to customers. The almost identical number of assignments yield double the revenue as the inbound cases.

But what pops off the chart is the amount of money per hour spent on the Open Source Intelligence (OSINT) up-sells or assignments. Half the revenue in the past 12 months came from OSINT - twice as much income as the outbound-marketed surveillance, and four times as much as inbound consumer-based surveillances. The most astonishing facet of this new-found business is that it is all organic. Word of mouth referrals, and getting into some well-heeled law firms and plush corporate board rooms.

She was marketing B2C and was making most of her money B2B with no end in sight. The OSINT has gone from a side hustle to paying hobby, to part-time and now threatening to go full-time. Beth is not sure how to proceed. Her business plan accounted for the growth of the surveillance business with an administrative assistant, Pat, and two more surveillance operatives working weekends to take the pressure off of Beth and Mary Chambers, her first hire, but nowhere did they plan for this cash cow.

John's Story: Pivot to B2C and then IMHF

John looked at his PI license differently now that he was a solo with Squire Investigations. He had to get a license 7 years earlier, when he started Independent Special Investigations, LLC. His goal then was to service the Property & Casualty Insurance industry, doing what he had done most of his career at the Police Department.

He was growing ISI to become a regional supplier of insurance fraud investigations from "Bangor to Baltimore." In the middle of that growth, two national firms seized competitive advantage and left John and many other local firms in their dust.

That PI license now came in handy for his phoenix to rise from the ashes.

He had a vague idea of what private investigators did, from talking to them when he made surveillance assignments back his days in SIU (Special Investigations Units). He began attending his local PI association more regularly and paying attention. He joined the National Association of Legal Investigators in 2004 and offered to teach a course at their annual conference in Indianapolis on Investigative Interviewing. It was eye-opening to see how many different specialists and experts were in attendance.

Most of the attendees were solo operators like him, but some worked with associates, and a handful owned large full-service firms. If money or people were involved in disputes, there was usually an attorney involved, and they needed a private investigator to get the facts to prevail in court.

He learned about a Los Angeles lawyer that specialized in Cable Piracy law. If a bar or lounge was showing a heavyweight fight without paying the cable operator for the rights to show it, they were stealing the feed.

The TV show "Cheaters" was offering franchises around the country. He had success with the piracy cases and luckily didn't pay a franchise fee for the Cheaters cases. Callers thought they would get their cases on the TV show for free.

He became one of the go-to PIs for other PIs around the country. He volunteered at the local courthouse, doing indigent intakes for the Public Defenders office when two investigators went out on sick leave and maternity leave. He tried his hand at skip-tracing.

John began cobbling together billable hours as a generalist. Lucky for him, Connecticut is a small state, and he still held his New York license as well. If customers wanted to pay him to go to NYC or Long Island, he could whistle a happy tune while he drove down and back.

He built an SEO-rich website and started receiving calls from the full spectrum of consumers, professionals, and businesses that needed his services.

He still had some clients from the ISI days, and those loyal clients formed the basis of his new business.

A local Criminal Defense attorney gave him a shot on a couple of small interview-intensive cases. She was then appointed by the court to handle the defense of a young man accused of murder. John began working that case at the state-appointed rate, which was less than 22% of his standard rate. He used these types of cases as "loss leaders" to get law firms to try him out, before trusting him with their larger, full-pay cases.

During this time, another lawyer hired him to find a missing heir. He gave John three weeks and a small budget. John exhausted both the time and money and when he asked for more of both, he was told no. But then the lawyer said, "Why don't you find her yourself?"

"Who will pay me?" John asked.

"You find her and convince her to give you a percentage of her inheritance in exchange for telling her where the estate is."

"Is that legal?" John asked.

He replied, "I will release you from the estate, and you are free to speculate on this case. It is called Missing Heir Research, and yes, it is legal and very lucrative."

John began learning Forensic Genealogy along with Criminal Defense investigation. His bag started filling up with missing heir and murder cases—an odd mix for sure.

He created a second DBA, Hoda Genealogy. John never found that heir, and it is still an open file on his desk. He started going to local Probate courts on Friday afternoons after he had met his billing goals for the week. He researched on nights and weekends. Over time, he had some successes and was able to do searches all day Friday. Then it became two days a week.

In April of 2008, John made as much from finding and signing heirs to one estate as the total of all his billable cases in 2007. He had a dozen other cases of variously projected payouts in the pipeline.

The murder case, mentioned earlier, went to trial in April. It was a three-week slugfest and, in the end, the young man was found not guilty in the first week of May 2008. John waited until after the celebration to tell the attorney he was moving on.

John decided to slowly disengage from Squire Investigations, to devote more time to Hoda Genealogy with a plan to go national. If it could work in Connecticut, he reasoned, why wouldn't his methods work around the country.

On Labor Day, 11 years to the day from his startup with ISI, John relaunched as International Missing Heir Finders, LLC.

Where Are You And Where Do You Want To Be?
An Expert can charge a premium for their time. What does it take for you to turn your specialties into expertise?
$500 an hour contracts are not unheard of.
$5,000 non-refundable retainers just to look at a serious problem is another.
Higher education, certifications, and a killer curriculum vitae may be in order. Who decides if you are an expert? Most of us do ponder what does it take to be an expert in court. A judge decides. What is that criteria? Who are court-admitted experts in your field?
Is it worth finding out you can take your specialty and elevate it to an area of expertise?
Appearing regularly on an Investigations reality TV series is another plus.
Anything with Forensic in your credentials is a plus.
Another excellent example of Expertise that does not have to be court-admissible is Background investigations for C-suite hires and mergers and acquisitions.
Bug sweeps and forensic examination of a cell phone, computer, and smart machines are two more examples.
An Expert PI company at the highest level of need for well-funded corporations, governmental agencies, or wealthy individuals brings together celebrity investigators and a vast network of contacts to the client. Think Bo Deitl, Kroll & Associates, and The Mintz Group.
What can you do in your little bustling burg to be that PI?

Hint-Marketing and Public Relations are the keys. A colleague of mine is experimenting with billboards. The message is mixed, but it's better than the thousands of dollars PIs wasted on yellow page ads–those were the business listings in the back of paper phone books, for you youngins' :)

How do you get the word out that, for anything investigative in your zip code, people should come to you first?

Join your local Chamber of Commerce and show up regularly. Join your State PI association and, after you make voluntary contributions to setting up meetings or conferences, throw your hat in the ring to get elected to a seat on the board. Here, you get to know who is good and who is not for your referral network.

Join a national Organization and make sure you spell out exactly what your skills sets are and the towns or cities where your car drives to regularly.

Offer to write articles for the association newsletter of your target audience in your state.

What webinars in your area of expertise will translate into continuing education credits for professionals in your bailiwick?

All of this builds credibility and, with a decent level of sales savvy, you can command a higher compensation because you are the expert in your area's large city.

A specialist crossing business segmentations by a skill set.
A stable surveillance company can cross business segmentation either B2B, P2P, or B2C. Can you create two-tier pricing that adds value to the B2B segment, such as two-car surveillance or a pre-surveillance and background check package?

How about Investigative Interviewing? Trial attorneys need written statements, Insurance companies need recorded statements, and Criminal Defense attorneys need both. Family Law and Unfair Employment Attorneys, ditto.

What do you do better than anyone else? Can you charge a premium because you are the best in your area? Can you train a staff up to your standards?

A Specialist with deep penetration in P2P, such as working exclusively for the niche of trial attorneys, or B2B such as insurance arson investigations (not an arson expert who can testify to Origin and Cause).

A Generalist working in a hard-to-reach geographical area. Aruba or Gig Harbor are just two examples. Showing up at International conferences and having a kick-ass SEO optimized website are two pre-requisites to become Magnum in Hawaii.

A Generalist competing on price, usually in the B2C world. Razor-thin profit margins have to be offset by volume and a lean fulfillment process. Be prepared to be a manager that has to fill in for employees who call-off sick.

Solo Generalist/Specialist with a few associates or part-timers. You have a steady amount of work coming in the door that pays the bills, and the workflow can be adjusted for busy or slack time.

Solo Generalist. Either your working your ass off or you have another source of income such as a pension or the means of pooling expenses with the other people in your personal life.

Sub-contractor or part-timer by choice for now. Maybe you are finishing school or working at another job and want to change your status sometime sooner than later.

SECTION TWO:
JUST DO IT.
INCREASE REVENUE.

$1,000 DAYS

Bill 4 hours at $250 per hour and you invoice $1,000.

Bill 6 hours at $170 per hour and you invoice $1,020.

Bill 8 hours at $125 per hour and you invoice $1,000.

Bill 10 hours at $100 per hour and you invoice $1,000.

Bill 14 hours at $75.00 per hour and you invoice $1,050.

First, how many $1,000-days do you need to make a living?

Jo needs to net $6,000 a month, after taxes of $3,000 a month, and $4,500 a month in businesses expenses, or $162,000 a year. Jo needs 162 days to cover costs. 172 days, if Jo wants to fund a $10,000 SEP IRA. That allows Jo to take five weeks of vacation (25 days), 12 holidays and every Wednesday (52), for 261 total work days a year. Jo doesn't work the weekends at all!

It seems far-fetched, doesn't it? The math is sound. It hinges on two premises: Jo is billing $1,000 every workday, but how much Jo charges per hour makes those billing days reasonable (6@ $170 per) or miserable (14@ $75 per). The obvious answer is that

Jo doesn't have to be miserable charging $75 per hour for services rendered. Jo just needs to staff up.

"But," you say, "what about marketing time, administrative time, non-billable travel time, and time spent on bookkeeping and accounting?"

On the 6-hour billing day, it is possible. On the 14-hour billing day, without help, it quickly becomes overwhelming.

I only have concentrated on the revenue side of the equation, and that is where I will stay. I am not here, in this book of the series, to tell you to clip coupons or forego an occasional meal. How you tighten your belt, both in your personal expenses and business expenses, places less pressure on your billing days. But that doesn't help you make $1,000 every working day.

Raise Rates. Just Do It.

All the arguments against raising rates are internal resistance or the gravity that weighs you down.

"But," you say, "my customers will leave me."

Not if you frame the increases like this:

- Announce a 10% increase for the New Year at Thanksgiving (or some other holiday to holiday period) and tell them they should get assignments to you before the price increase takes effect.
- The following year, round up to hourly rates to the next number ending with a zero. For example: $115 becomes $120.
- Add a new feature to each of your flat rates to justify the increase. Tell your customers how that new feature helped a client, with a testimonial from that client. A $299 flat rate with this new and improved feature is now a $350 flat rate.

- Rush assignments and holidays are premium times. Clients understand the concept of overtime. (Although I went to a bowling alley last night, a Friday night, to interview witnesses on an Indigent court-appointed case at $35 an hour. It is necessarily a favor for an old client. All the witnesses I needed to talk to were there, and none of them were favorable to his client.)

I have raised rates several times. I had to have this advice pounded in my hard head, not once, but twice.

I didn't lose any good customers. I lost the burners and the grinders. I didn't go out of business by raising rates. I began to get paid for the real value I gave to my clients.

This advice fits here, and it may be the only time in this book of the series that I offer marketing advice.

Six weeks before your planned vacation of more than a week, you contact your top clients and tell them of your plans. They will ask where you are going and for how long. Your call acts as a tickle for them to get off their patoot and send you over that file that has been sitting there on their desk collecting dust.

But Don't Stop There

Go into your database of clients (CRM) or assignment log of who gave you work last year, but haven't called this year. Leave messages with them telling them of your upcoming vacation plans.

It is a non-threatening call, and it is a great way to re-establish contact. It results in more work from people that are again your clients.

The added benefit of this call is that your clients will respect you more. They will value you for the professional that you are.

You are giving them the courtesy of telling them how to avoid the emergency assignment later on. They will respect you for being able to take a vacation. They see you are organized and trying to lead a balanced life. This is part of why you can charge what you do.

It's a subtle reminder your time is valuable.

One-Time Customers

"What are your rates?" "How much do you charge an hour." You get asked almost immediately. You haltingly, and with a catch in your voice, answer with your customer-friendly per-hour rate. You hope they don't nickel and dime you.

Don't do that. Don't do that ever again.

According to one of my closest mentors, Jimmie Mesis, former owner of PI Magazine, the answer is two very simple words:

"It depends."

That is the ledge for you to start asking questions about the case.

"What have you already done?"

"When do you need it by?

"Is there anything more I need to know about."

"What is the outcome you are looking for?"

But here is where the magic comes in.

You ask, "What have you set aside for the matter?" The other way to phrase it differently is, "What is your budget?"

In response to either answer, you sigh and say, "Tell you what, I will be able to do at least X,Y, and Z first for (slightly less than the amount they named), and we'll see where that gets us." If you priced it right, you have a budget for far much more per hour than if you quoted your hourly rate and did all the steps. You can get authorization for more money if the next steps bring them closer to their goals.

If they come back really low, tell them you will not be able to do it for that amount, but you have somebody who may be willing to do it for that price. However, there is no guarantee of success. Go back over their needs, overcome the price objection with your offer again, and ask, "That sounds reasonable to me, what do you think?"

Retainers

I take retainers from everybody except for in-state attorneys and regulars.

On complicated cases where putting together a couple of flat rates isn't even a suggestion, I tell them I work on refundable retainers of $5,000. I can send them the retainer agreement, and when I receive the funds, I start putting together the case. It could be as much as 40 hours of work on a homicide case or 20 hours of work to try and find heirs in Slovenia ($125-$250 per hour). I have a real incentive to be super-efficient with my time. The takeaway for you is this:

Divide the number of hours you think the case should take into $5,000. That answer should be more than your hourly rate. Don't be greedy, but it should be more. Two things happen here. First, you get paid up front and don't have to chase the money. Second, you are working the case for a premium, and you didn't sell yourself short (again). Send them a report with your results with the little bit of left-over money or apply the money to the next retainer. They will be happy with your results if you stay within budget, hopefully–definitely, with a return of some money.

Stop Discounting

Always round up, not down, when you figure out what your budget will be. Always think 1.1 to 1.25 times your average rate. You can handle surprises on the street much better that way.

Give a volume discount when you get the volume.

Suppose I have three interviews lined up with witnesses at the same location. I have a flat rate for signed statements. I invoice for 2.5 statements. My client is happy, and I am ecstatic. I didn't have to drive to and from three separate statements.

Clients sometimes promise a lot of volume, when they haven't paid you for the first and only case that you have. Politely, tell them the price will change when the volume comes in. Period.

Don't discount for taking ApplePay, PayPal, or charge cards. You have set up systems for your clients to pay you conveniently. That is their benefit.

Stop Giving Stuff Away For Free

Except for When You Will Make A Ton Of Money By Rewarding Great Customers, Or In A Targeted Marketing Campaign.

Framing the conversation around this issue is not tricky. If you need to clinch the deal, throwing in extras is not the way to close. Continue to talk about their need and your value. They will respect you more for holding your ground. You are worth every penny they will pay you. This begs the question: how much do you need their business? Part of getting to making $1,000 every working day is the ability to be selective. That you have so much in the pipeline, you can afford to be picky.

Mary is frantic. She calls you up and says they can't find their client who has to be served for a deposition the Tuesday after an upcoming holiday weekend. It's late Friday afternoon. You say hold on. You just happen to be in your favorite low-cost database.

A) You pull up the client's new cell phone, and you get the client on the phone while Mary is listening on the other line. You tell the client that Mary, from their law firm, will call in a few minutes. Mary is ecstatic. You tell Mary you love working for them and the reasons why. You just pulled a rabbit out of a hat and best of all;

you tell her because you value their business so much, you are happy to do this one for free.

B) You pull up the client's new cell phone, call the client, and make the connection. It took you five minutes. You call Mary back and tell her the client is waiting for her call, and you will be sending the bill over Saturday morning for your usual LOCATE flat rate she is accustomed to. Mary is grateful.

You decide which is more important to you. I personally like doing magic - it's more fun. I can make money mostly every working day.

Fire Customers

	Fast paying	Slow paying
High paying	H+F	H+S
Low paying	L+F	L+S

You can, and you should, fire customers.

The first to go are the low-paying and slow-paying clients. You are better off using that time to market and up-sell your high-paying and fast-paying clients.

"But, but," you sputter, "how do I turn away that work? It's steady. It fills up my work days."

Think about your goal of making $1,000 every working day.

You are dragging an anchor under your sailboat.

Plan a date to politely start telling them that you are jammed up with your other cases. You may try to rehabilitate them by saying you need them to send you $X with the assignments from now on. They then become good-paying-fast-paying clients. If they balk, cut loose that anchor before it snags on the bottom.

I did this with an insurance company that only paid for 4-hour time blocks of surveillance with no drive time or mileage. I made money with their work by hiring part-timers from the local Criminal Justice graduate program. Their cameras were not expensive, and neither was the video download programs. We made report templates and, like the organized chaos of Lucy and Ethel on the chocolate drop assembly line, we handled their work, but at an emotional cost.

The claim representatives would pay when they felt like it and nitpicked constantly. They made up 20% of my revenue, but when you subtracted out all of the overhead and my time, the aggravation was not worth it. Firing them was liberating. It freed me up to use that administrative time to find better clients, and I did.

Next to go are the low-paying fast-paying client. That is a harder sell, I know.

This is the predicament Beth Clark has with her inbound marketing of infidelity investigations surveillance. They pay the bills, they absorb overhead, and they keep people on the payroll, but they chew up her time. Time she could spend with high-paying clients that pay on time, or those she has to send an occasional reminder to.

By offering flat rate blocks of time with no extras, she has packaged a service to be a commodity. There is nothing wrong with commoditizing a service. If you can scale it, it can be profitable. This why it is so tempting for Beth to keep offering this service. She figured out how to do inbound marketing while her competitors were writing on the cave walls. This repeatable and scalable business does offer her great value if she could move out of operations and fulfillment, or sell this lucrative piece.

It took me a while to get around to asking you this question: **What is your time worth?**

This may be the reason for most of your resistance and the gravity that holds you down. If you are going to settle for grinding out hours, and spending hours administrating those hours to barely keep your head above water, you have to ask yourself why.

I find a witness that says my quadriplegic client had the green light while the police throw their hands up in the air about who was at fault.

I go to the crime scene and realize it was impossible for the State's star witness to see the client commit the murder. After I confronted her, she tells me she was making it up based on cues from the detectives.

What is my time worth to the disabled person, or the defendant, both facing a lifetime of misery? What was the result worth to the attorney paying my bill?

What is my time worth to the business customer who has a problem if my results solve their problem? It might be worth X to them. If they went with the cheaper and less-effective competitor they might pay less for per hour, they run the higher risk of still having to pay X.

These are the questions you have to ask yourself, and even ask the client when they hem and haw at your quote. Don't underestimate your value to the client. They can do a good enough job of that for you. Part of your sales technique is to help them realize why you and your company are the best fit. You are worth it.

Understand that a gourmet restaurant and McDonald's both serve food. Don't confuse the different customers' expectations. But that does bring me to the next heading. "Do you want fries with that shake?"

SECTION TWO: JUST DO IT. INCREASE REVENUE

Up-sell and Affiliate Marketing
I still do not do enough up-selling.

Straightforward example: I am asked by a client to go to an accident scene and find security cameras that may have captured the events on video.

I go there twice if the accident happened after hours. During the daytime, I visit the business establishments (when the owners would be most likely be there) to talk them into sharing their video feeds.

Then, I go to the scene again on the same day of the week, at the same time of day as the accident, to canvas for witnesses. My clients are happy with my results.

But what if I suggested that we ask, under the Freedom of Information Act, for the 911 caller audio tapes and the body cams or dashboard cams of the responding officer?

That up-sell gives value for which I can charge more, and we might also identify additional witnesses not listed on the police report, which can be a further up-sell.

Do you know how many of those 911 callers tipped the scale in favor of my attorney's client? I am learning to make that up-sell at the time of the assignment.

Always lock down the original assignment first, then talk about the value add.

"I normally charge X for this, but since I am already (in the data) (at the scene) (over by the courthouse) (whatever your upsell is), I can do it for 85% of Y. Makes sense to me, what do you think?"

Here is the fun part. In my assignment log, I note the up-sell in with a check mark in the up-sell column and then type in the dollar amount in the money field right next to it. Every quarter,

I total the up-sell dollars. Can you do this on the road to making $1,000 every working day?

Look at every service you provide. How can you up-sell them?

"Do you want a background check with that shake?"

"Do you want an asset check with that shake?"

"Would you like me to run a search for Y while I am in the data with that shake?"

If the kid at the McDonald's register can do that, why can't you?

If the server at the fancy restaurant can ask, "We have a special on Harvey Wall Bangers, can I start you out with one?" Why can't you?

> There was a time when I charged clients $3.00 a page for transcription. My business, at the time, was very report-heavy and all my people dictated reports. I paid less than $1.75 a page to an overnight transcription firm. I was able to take my family of four to a warm weather vacation every February from charging that extra $1.25. Charles Dickens didn't have anything on me! I didn't have a single B2B client complain about my transcription costs. It was part of the territory. However, in the P2P world, my clients want more flat rates instead of itemized bills, and I adjusted.

Affiliate Marketing

You can't be an expert in everything. When your clients call you for an assignment that is way beyond your skill sets, you tell them you can't help them, sorry.

Wrong!

You instead connect them to your good friend Ryan or Terry, who have the expertise and the proven track record. They can do the job, and for the referral, Terry or Ryan will send you a percentage of the fee as a referral fee. What is 20% of $5,000? You just made your $1,000 for that working day by taking a phone call and making a phone call. Of course, you have worked hard to earn the trust of your client and spent considerable time culling a group of experts to surround yourself with.

USABugSweeps.com is a great example. This is where I formally introduce you to my friend and mentor of two decades. Jimmie Mesis is recognized as an expert in the field of residential and business Technical Surveillance Countermeasures (TSCM) bug sweeps. He has been associated with the field of TSCM for more than 35 years and conducts several hundred sweeps every year throughout the United States and abroad. He has a referral program for PIs around the world. What a great marketing idea.

Here are other experts for example

- Accident re-constructionist
- Forensic computer and cell phone recovery for data extraction or recovery from digital devices
- Handwriting experts
- Recovering data from security cameras
- Skip Tracing
- Arson Investigator

- Forensic Genealogist
- Forensic (Fill in the blank)

This list is by no means exhaustive. The idea is merely to have your clients come to you for all their needs. If you have targeted your audience carefully, your specialization will align with their needs. Experts or other sources are just a phone call away for you. Or you could have your clients call your competitors. Your choice.

*A client needed to locate their ex-wife in St. Maarten, this past January. I jokingly offered to go, but then I did the next best thing. I went into my INTELLENET directory and emailed three investigators on the Dutch side of that Caribbean island. Two got back to me quickly and took the time to talk it over with me. I forwarded both of their contacts to the client, who ended up choosing one. I didn't take a fee from either of them, but I charged the client for an hour, which he happily paid. I now know two good PIs for everything St. Maarten.

Hint: Going to national conferences or super regional conferences like FALI, TALI and CALI or the SuperConference Jimmie Mesis put on every other year is a great way to learn about the latest technologies from vendors wanting to do a free demo for you, meeting folks from all over the world, and learning from experts. I come back from EVERY conference with something that will make me money immediately, and it always offsets the cost of being away from my billing days and the expenses associated with the travel.

I budget for two conferences a year. I recommend you do at least one.

SECTION TWO: JUST DO IT. INCREASE REVENUE

SECTION THREE: WEARING FEWER HATS

EMBRACE YOURSELF–REPLACE YOURSELF

The job functions you shed depends on your customer segmentation. Your labor intensity and the degree of specialization of your service plays a factor, as well. Some assignments are more burdensome on your administrative shoulders than others.

It has been my experience that Professional Investigators let go and sometimes actually drop the ball on the wrong functions first. When most PIs get busy, they stop marketing and then hire someone to help with the investigations (Fulfillment) when in reality it is much better to hire a part-time bookkeeper to do the books. (You still control the checkbook.)

Do you think I wake up on a beautiful Saturday morning looking forward to sitting with my bookkeeper, doing the books and reconciling the credits cards with QuickBooks? Not really, but it does allow me to spend time during the week wearing other hats.

In B2C and B2B, an administrative assistant can be trained to take in cases from the inbound marketing and callers. Your AA can open cases, assign investigators, maintain a diary on the cases to make sure none get dropped or delayed, put the reports together, and send you the reports for invoicing (again, no one entity in your operation handles every process altogether).

You think the time you are no longer spending on keystroking accounts payable and maintaining the assignment log among other administrative chores can be spent on investigations.

Wrong!

That time is better-spent marketing. Then you go on to hiring and training people to do fulfillment. You have to fill the pipeline to have others handle fulfillment.

The goal of making $1,000 every working day is met by having enough cases in the pipeline to plan your $1,000 working day for the week ahead, or maybe even into the following week, on your scheduled appointments.

This is where resistance and drag intersect to keep you for propelling into orbit. You want to hold on to investigations because that is what you like and that is what you are better at.

The first thing PIs who own their businesses give up is Marketing, and that is not to be given up but has to be expanded if you wish to maintain and grow. There is no such thing as lifetime customers. Customers come and go. How do you replace customers that leave if you are no longer marketing? How do you plan to grow if you are not marketing to more prospects, and better-paying prospects?

I would rather investigate. I would instead canvas a crime scene in the Projects on that sun-splashed Saturday morn, then work on the client newsletter. So it took me a long time to appreciate the value of marketing.

You have to then add investigators, to where you have so many investigators that you hire an investigations supervisor and get off the street and out of fulfillment. This is where most PIs stop. They don't hire the investigations supervisor, and they don't hire a full-time marketing person. Yes, hiring to handle bookkeeping and administrative services make the load much lighter. Replacing some investigative time with some combination of sub-contractors, part-timers, and full-timers help the bottom line, and you can pick and choose your cases, and the ones that you want to ride along on for supervisory or quality control reasons.

Your internal resistance and the drag of carrying a load of a team now keeps you from getting into space. Part of your resistance is the mistaken belief that when you or somebody along with you increases the marketing effort, you are paying for unnecessary overhead.

How could anybody be productive 40 hours a week marketing your little company? It goes back to the original misconception that if you do good work, you will always be busy. Many PIs fail to grasp the obvious. X number of hours marketing or working on marketing functions produces a multiple of X in billable hours of investigation. Marketing types will say you can exponentially increase your yield by constantly tweaking your message.

For example, one year, I set out to increase my billable hours to 35 hours a week for myself and a new part-timer. Doesn't sound like much, but when you are billing an average of $150 an hour, you are making $1,050 every working day.

Marketing less than 5 hours a week, I was able to achieve that goal consistently. Imagine a 7-to-1 ratio of billable hours to marketing hours. Here is the rub: you didn't form your investigations company to become a full-time marketer, and the thought of having to hire and manage a full-time marketer places you way outside your comfort zone. It goes back to your root assumptions that you want to grow your investigative skill sets and not your marketing skills.

SECTION THREE: WEARING FEWER HATS

At 2pm next Thursday, you have two webinars going off at the same time. One is "Better Background Checks," and the other is "How 2 A/B test your CTA (Call to Actions)." Which one is going to capture your eyeballs? I thought so.

Which one will have a more significant impact on your bottom line? You know the answer.

This false ceiling of mindset keeps the owner in fulfillment and marketing is done on a catch-as-catch-can basis. This is the bane of most small business owners and not just PI firms.

Stay With Me On This

You then hire a part-time marketer to expand your pipeline even further to where you could promote from within your probationary investigations supervisor.

You are now managing a bookkeeper, an administrative assistant, a part-time marketer, and an investigations supervisor. You outsource IT and the managing of your website, but you still can add content, if you wish.

You still plan the marketing and do the quality control of the investigations, and you still oversee field training. The billings have to absorb all that overhead from the people that don't bill files. You have to watch the right numbers (metrics) and make sure you are strategically aligned with them.

If you have done your planning right, you can go out on the cases you want to work with your staff and still take that trip to Paris you have wanted to do for years.

You then promote from within a Director of Administration, Marketing and Operations.

That is how you build a business that runs without you but remember, you always oversee the checkbook.

That is a good exercise, and for many people, it is something worth aspiring to.

However, more practically, I want to return to the proposition of making $1,000 every working day. We will apply these ideas to each Customer Segmentation below towards making sure you are meeting your goal.

The weekend after completing the five-year plan, Tony does his invoicing and looks at the quarterlies. He compares how much he made this quarter to the previous quarter. He compares his billable hours from Criminal Defense to Business Investigations. He compares them to the previous quarter by segment. Then he made the same comparisons to the same quarter last year. Criminal Defense was not even in the same quarter in his first year. He compares flat rates to hourly cases to budgets and retainers. He saw which upsells were working and which ones weren't.

He is growing exponentially—in layperson terminology: by leaps and bounds. He could easily afford a part-time administrative assistant who could do light bookkeeping. That position could grow into full-time as he added more investigators. He had been tracking his Admin and BK time and saw that it averaged 15 hours a week. Before he even launched Russo & Associates, he started tracking his time, and it was an ingrained habit. After getting the admin up and running, he would devote five of those hours to more marketing, five to recruiting and hiring associates and he would give himself five hours off and plan to do something for himself on these precious days. He has been sprinting

SECTION THREE: WEARING FEWER HATS

work-wise for months now, and it is time to get back in the gym three days a week.

One of the people from his Chamber of Commerce meetings wants to spend more time at home with their kids and left their job as an executive assistant. Tony pitches the job to them and aside from two hours every other Saturday at Tony's office for bookkeeping, they can work remotely. They shake hands on it.

Two detectives from Tony's old squad are looking to work part-time in retirement. They are happier than tall dogs in a meat store to work with him as associates.

That Associate thing on the website and business cards is now going to pay off, he thinks.

In short order, they get their PI licenses, Insurances and become "1099" sub-contractors. They are free to refuse cases. They are free to work the cases the way they want, when they want, and how they want to. They are free to work for other PIs, after signing non-competes and non-disclosure agreements with Tony. Abe and Tony's accountant makes sure they are genuinely sub-contractors. Tony nets 60% after expenses on their 20 hours a week each, which gave him more breathing room, even with the increased emphasis on marketing.

One morning after a client arraignment, Abe pulls Tony aside. "Tony, I want you to meet somebody." He said.

Abe motions to the man who walks over to them with an uneven gait.

Tony shakes hands with the man who is half his age. The grip is strong, and the eyes are clear, and they don't look away. As Tony takes him in, he sees an over-developed upper body and the tell-tale sign of a prosthesis where a lower right leg had been.

Abe doesn't miss a beat. "Joe was on a foot beat in Brooklyn when an uninsured and unlicensed drunk lost control of his car and pinned Joe up against a wall."

"Abe tells me you are good people and that you were "real police" when you were on the job," Joe says.

"He's been handling some of my process serving while he finishes his rehab and is now ready for some steady work," Abe adds.

"How do you feel about Abe and I working for criminal defendants?" Tony asks point blank.

Joe shrugs. "I miss the work, but not the BS. I never got a chance to go after my gold shield. I was slated for a plain-clothes detail until this happened." He pointed to where the pants cuff touches the right shoe. "I figure this would be the best way to use my brains. We both know that the cops don't always get it perfect. I've watched you guys from the gallery a few times, and I liked what I saw."

"Before you decide Joe, why don't you ride with me a few days and if you like it, we can do a 60-day probationary period. Whaddya think?"

"I'd like that." The smile was wide and grateful.

SECTION THREE: WEARING FEWER HATS

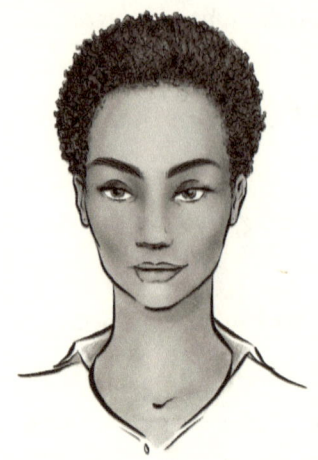

Beth decides to split her operations. Mary Chambers consistently steers business away or into the 4- and 6-hour blocks. However, she is the perfect trainer and field supervisor for the newly hired surveillance operatives. In very short order, they had to hire even a few more. Beth gave Mary more responsibility with the surveillance teams while diverting Mary's marketing calls to Pat, the administrative assistant, who converts better on the inbound calls and for more 6- and 8-hour blocks.

Pat is full-time and will soon be overseeing a burgeoning business that grew out of online dating.

Background checks on prospective spouses have increased. Beth and Pat create a template for them, just in time to capitalize on a marketing stream generated from Internet Dating.

Truth Be Told Investigations, Inc is getting assignments from all over the country to do backgrounds on the persons that the well-to-do prospect are going to meet for their first date after connecting on an internet dating site.

Where online access to criminal records is blocked in individual states and the subject does not leave any social media footprints, the clients are advised that when Jack or Jill lived in that other state, they can not report without hiring a field investigator to access the records and do the background in person.

Beth devotes a landing page just for Internet Dating background checks, offers a free report in exchange for the prospect's email and streams voice testimonials from clients who were adequately warned. The thankfulness just gushes over the phone.

Beth can hire a full-time background checker who also handles inbound calls, as well.

Beth continues to market to the upscale woman's market in the Greater Austin, TX area now that she is not pulling surveillance shifts. She rotates different operatives with her on the marketing visits and finds one operative to be particularly adept at learning how to make the pitch.

Sam took marketing courses in college and understood what Beth is trying to do. Beth rides along with Sam as Sam markets to businesses catering to upscale women in the surrounding counties. With a growing population, the area is now supporting over 2 million people. Sam quickly goes to half-time as a marketer and half-time doing surveillance.

Although Beth is not on the street anymore, she and Mary randomly show up at surveillance sites to check on their people, especially on the one-car surveillances.

When an operative was fired for falsifying time sheets, word got around that somebody is watching the watchers.

That is not to say that Beth is resting on her laurels. She continues to grow her OSINT business, and with help from Pat and the full-time background checker, it can stand alone.

She finds it very elusive training them to her level of expertise. Much of their work is routinized, and her case management system allows them to collaborate real-time and more importantly, for them to work remotely.

She looks hard at this business and realizes that she needs to tap into other intelligence professionals if she wants to grow it.

What was it? She has grown out of her Truth Be Told brand for this lucrative side business.

SECTION THREE: WEARING FEWER HATS

She needs to rebrand if she wants to position her new business effectively in the market place. She has to learn how to market this B2B market without leaning on the law firms that handle TBT clients Family Law and Divorce cases.

How can she replicate and scale this organic growth?

Barely four years after leaving the Armed Guard business, Beth is at the crossroads again. Her goal was to build Truth Be Told to be sold, but what about this new bright shiny object that her proof of concept shows to be a cash cow?

The offer stuns her and changes everything. Her old employer sees the value of her company and how when combined with the acquisition of a security firm would create a B2C and B2B powerhouse.

Where Beth had not wanted to dilute her brand with doing corporate and insurance surveillance, her former employer is ideally positioned to capitalize on her people's advance surveillance skills and a support infrastructure to go with it.

The deal will be paid out over three years. This year's revenue will be matched up front, and half of each of the next two years' revenues will be paid to her monthly with a guaranteed monthly minimum.

Beth will receive two-plus years of revenue spread out over three years. Business valuations for her business say this is a premium offer and she should take it.

She can bank the payouts and accelerate her plans to retire early to go on adventure travel trips, while she bootstraps her way into the OSINT B2B world.

Her former employer's contacts with the Banking, Energy, and growing Corporate headquarters scene of Austin is her toehold into that B2B where her new buyer has nurtured contacts for years. It is very gratifying to see how her hard work and professionalism is appreciated. Her buyer is making out well. She has built a turnkey operation that will open the doors on a B2C world for them with her proven inbound marketing plan.

There are a lot of tears and hugs at the year-end holiday party for Truth Be Told Investigations, when Beth tells her staff about the changes that will take place in the next couple of weeks. She has to cancel her travel plans between Christmas and New Years to finish the valuation for sale and to complete her business plan for Clark Intelligence Solutions, LLC.

SECTION THREE: WEARING FEWER HATS

John expanded his new company, International Missing Heir Finders, LLC into New York, New Jersey, Massachusetts, and Rhode Island. He hired two people to visit probate courts in those surrounding states on a weekly schedule, to look for files where people had died without a will, and where the possibility of missing heirs existed.

He had competitive advantage in CT and hired a full-time genealogist to carry much of the load while he handled the sales (signing heirs to contracts) and he oversaw the attorneys until the cases paid off.

John's fledgling company scored big on a case where ten cousins kinda-sorta forgot they had two half-aunts and a half-uncle with whom they had grown up, and John discovered. IMHF signed them up, and the courts agreed that those ten cousins were not entitled to a dime. John's heirs would take the whole estate.

Finally, when the money came in from that estate, John could roll out a national expansion. He hired a marketing rep and marketing company to help him with the rollout. He hired a full-time Administrative Assistant and implemented a custom-made Case Management System.

A dozen reality-TV producers pursued him, and one followed John around for two days just before Christmas around Columbia, South Carolina, and Milford, CT to create a "sizzle reel" that they shopped to the Oprah, Discovery and TLC channel.

John hoped to have local genealogists scout out cases in the rural counties around the country as his experience was beginning to show that his firm were guppies swimming in the shark pool of most urban areas. John wanted to follow the "Tracer" model of other forensic genealogists and pay the tracers 10% of what he received after his attorneys took their fees.

International Missing Heir Finders attended the genealogy conferences around the country and made its pitch. The marketing rep cold-called genealogists who lived near the county seats in those rural counties. More urban counties were going online with probate filings, and more searching was done online.

One Sunday morning, John found an estate in Memphis, Tennessee. It looked strange with only a niece coming forward. In their research, they found that she was actually a "niece-in-law" and was not entitled to a penny.

They found and signed up 34 of 35 cousins. They also hired per diem sub-contractors for target-rich areas which did not appear to be shark-infested. Missing heir research is a highly competitive business. John learned quickly where not to swim. The infrastructure was completed with the hire of another desk genealogist.

The goal was to fill the pipeline with so many cases. The far-and-few-between large pay-outs would be buttressed by a steady stream of smaller and mid-size cases. He planned to grow the business to effectuate an employee buy-out in 2017 with a gradual three-year payout to 2020.

SECTION FOUR: HIRING

TAKE THE BLINDFOLD OFF

Unless you plan to boost your business by commanding an expert's compensation or have a highly-specialized team of associates, you will need to hire full time or part-time personnel. You will have to offset their costs and the increase in overhead with even more billable hours. The time to recruit, hire, train, supervise, evaluate, and fire (don't think you are immune from bad hires) takes away from other time you spend wearing your other hats, including fulfillment. So you will have to have them shoulder part of your load as well.

Hire slow and fire fast. The recruiting and hiring function is crucial when building a business. A wrong hire compounds the time needed to correct the situation and make a proper hire, usually at a time when the time is short supply and high demand.

SECTION FOUR: HIRING

Doing an autopsy on a lousy hire usually reveals:

- What the prior employers couldn't tell you. Ask, "Who else can I talk to who worked with you but no longer works there?"
- What references gloss over on work history. They feign ignorance of parts of their friend's life. Ask, "Can I interview your best friend?" If the applicant balks, ask why.
- Other past employers not listed on the resume and skipped over on the application.
- You, yes you, glossed over the red flags staring you in the face on the pre-interview questionnaire and during the oral interview.
- Glaring discrepancy between what was thought to be job-specific experience and performance, especially after you train them to perform satisfactorily.
- Tardiness, absenteeism, lateness on work and report completion.
- A relapse in alcohol or drug addiction that now explains the previous gaps in employment. To anyone who has recruited and hired employees, it only takes one or two Dr. Jekyll and Mr. Hyde experiences to see what this behavior looks like. Unfortunately, it happens too often in Small Businesses as the applicant thinks they can fool a small business owner who does not have formalized hiring practice.
- They could hide in a larger organization, but now the spotlight is glaring on them in your small business. Ensure the oral interview includes questions on projects and team involvement. This employee is going to be working on YOUR project and YOUR Team now.
- You didn't train them well, and they could not overcome your lousy training. That one hurts.

- You run your business like Spanky's clubhouse and have demotivated a person that held real promise. Every day is a Chinese fire drill at your office. They quit and tell you why they are quitting. They pull no punches. That hurts worse.
- The lack of process and procedure place an undue burden on performance.
- There is no consistency in their supervision.
- A non-existent performance appraisal process is compounded by always catching them underperforming. Sometimes praise has to be muttered as part of the appraisal process.

Beth came from the Army, Tony from NYPD, and John was once a manager with multi-national insurance and financial giant AIG. Previously only John had the flexibility of selecting staff, but all three were experienced in supervision and performance appraisal.

Take responsibility for a bad hire. The sooner you see you failed to make the best possible choice you could or provide them with a workplace where they had a chance to succeed, the sooner you can fix the problem, because it IS your problem to fix. Here are some tools that you can use.

New Hire Checklist
Employment Application

- Personal information
- Employment Desired
- Education
- Employment History
- Additional Information
- proof of citizenship
- can you perform all essential functions of a job

- Any accommodations or workplace modifications needed?
- Authorizations for Credit, Driver's history and Criminal Background.

Pre-Interview Questionnaire

- What is the number one reason you want this job?
- How can you make a difference at our company?
- What are the three most important things you think our company does every day?
- If you've ever been fired, tell us what happened:
- What makes for satisfying work experience?
- Tell us something you are excited about?
- Where do you see your career five years from now?

Interview Questionnaire

- What brings you here today?
- Tell me about yourself?
- What events from your childhood shaped who you are today?
- Tell me three or four things of which you are most proud.
- What is the most important thing to you about any job?
- What were the most significant contributions in your current and previous jobs?
- What are your natural strengths?
- What do you like doing best?
- What are some of your natural weaknesses?
- What do you like doing the least?
- Tell me about some of the most important projects you have ever worked on? At least one that worked out and one that didn't (job by job)

- What was your most exciting work experience in the past five years?
- What was your worst work experience in the past five years? How did you contribute to this scenario?
- Who is the best (investigator) you have ever met
- What is the greatest challenge that you've had to overcome in your work career?
- What is the most significant opportunity that you "blew" in your work career?
- Please describe something that felt unfair at your previous place of employment?
- Tell me about a time when you had a conflict with (a boss, subordinate, co-workers). How did you resolve it?

Receipt Of Hire Letter Acceptance

- Hire Letter; may reference the position contract (below)
    - Appointment
    - Remuneration
    - Performance Reviews
    - Probationary period
- Signed Employment Application
- W-4 for tax withholding
- I-9 copies for permanent file
- Employee Handbook Signature Page
- Equipment inventory sign off
- Non-Compete Agreement
- Business cards
- Sign up and passwords for databases
- Association memberships

- Workers Compensation addition and correct job classification
- Errors and Omission addition to policy
- Timesheet sample

Employee Handbook

- Welcome page
- Acknowledgment Page
- Equal Opportunity
- Employment Classification: Full time, Part time, Temporary, 1099
- Confidentiality Clause
- Personal Information
- Attendance
- Work Hours
- Overtime–Overtime work is only performed when approved in advance by your supervisor. You are expected to work mandatory overtime when requested to do so, and you will receive time and one-half regular pay for the time exceeding forty (40) hours in the given work week.
- Lunch period
- Safety and accident rules
- Use of company property - person use exclusion
- Use of company computers
- Substance Abuse Policy
- Sexual Harassment
- Performance & Salary Reviews
- Payroll
- Holidays

- Vacation
- Sick Leave
- Maternity Leave
- Funeral Leave
- Jury Duty
- Time off for school conferences
- Time off for voting
- Military Service
- Group Insurance
- Continuation of Medical/ COBRA Insurance
- Workers Compensation
- Educational Assistance
- Layoff and Recall
- Termination of employment

Position Contract

Can be used instead of an employment application.

- Job Title
- Location
- Reports to:
- Pay Rate
- Performance Review Date:
- Type of Position: FT, PT Contractor, Intern
- Results to be achieved by this position (Expected outcomes and Performance Measures)
- Standards for this position (standards of Excellence)
- Work requirements for this position (Duties, Responsibilities, Accountabilities)

SECTION FOUR: HIRING

- Success Factors
- Analytical thinking
- Business knowledge
- Communications/ Listening
- Company Knowledge
- Critical Thinking
- Customer Focus
- Decision Making
- Leadership
- Organization
- People Development
- Resilience/Flexibility
- Results Orientation
- Team Building
- Teamwork
- Functional Excellence
- Company Values
- Experience needed for a position
- Other/special requirements for this position

Policies and Procedures

See Employee Handbook

TAKE THE BLINDFOLD OFF

SECTION FIVE:
DO AS I SAY AND AS I DO

TRAINING TO COMPETENCY

It starts with the textbooks such as these examples:

- *Fundamentals of Criminal Investigation* by Charles O'Hara, Gregory O'Hara
- *Uncovering Reasonable Doubt: The Component Method* by Brandon A. Perron
- *Casualty, Fire and Marine Investigation Checklists-9th* by Ken Brownlee and Pat Magarik
- *Memory-Enhancing Techniques for Investigative Interviewing: The Cognitive Interview* by Ronald P Fisher and R. Edward Geiselman
- *Tracing Missing Heirs* by Ralph D Thomas
- *Code of Professional Conduct (2006 ed.)* by Kitty Hailey, CLI
- *Techniques of Legal Investigations* by Anthony M. Golec

These are just a few on my bookshelf. What's on your bookshelf or e-reader?

Subscriptions:

- *PI Magazine* by Publishers Nicole Cusanelli and Jim Nanos

- *Data2Know* by Cynthia Hetherington, The Hetherington Group

Next, come the Checklists.

Have they been written down and given to each trainee?

Examples:

- Statement guides
- Surveillance preparations and protocols
- Scene Diagrams, Photos, and Measurements
- Location steps
- Skip-tracing steps
- Background steps

If it is a repetitive task, create a workflow process. Learn it yourself, discuss best practices with peers, minimize mistakes by rigid analysis and continuous self-improvement.

Continue your education with seminars, webinars, and classes.

Have the trainee ride with you to observe best practices. Don't throw them out there on their own with a wave. "Just do A, B, and C and bring back 1, 2, and 3." They will go to the store for lettuce and sometimes come back with cabbage.

Allow the trainee enough situations to create a replicable pattern. One-and-done is a recipe for disaster. Think about the repair garage owner training a new mechanic on how to install brakes. Don't you want the owner over the mechanic's shoulder as they work on brakes for the first time, and maybe the second time, and even the third?

Observe the trainee undertake the interview, the surveillance, or investigation under your direct supervision to reinforce the training. You may have to jump in to assist, but the frequency and depth should decrease over time. You have to allow minor, correctable mistake-making. They are still painting by numbers and will go outside the lines. It won't be a DaVinci the first time they pick up the paintbrush. It wasn't for you either, when you first started.

Offer feedback and continue to seek out situations where you can ride along to cement the learning and minimize bad habits from forming.

Can you distill the textbooks and checklists into training modules for your employees? The caseload is not only there to be worked through. It offers you a plethora of chances to build the foundation of the employee's investigative skills.

Replicable satisfactory performance is the goal.

What I see most times, with other PI firms, is that training is transactional and not transformative. The "what we do" gets passed on, but the foundational "why we do it" does not. You can fiddle with your smartphone or talk about how your team blew the lead on your ride-along, or you can plan the windshield time to reinforce the teaching from similar cases. Explain why you do things that way and not the wrong way. You are teaching the skill, but you are also teaching critical thinking. At some point, that trainee will be an employee out on their own.

Do you want them to be able to react quickly and think on their feet?

Example: A personal injury attorney asks you to secure an affidavit of no insurance from the owner/operator of a striking vehicle. Knowing why you are doing that task helps you deal with that person when they would rather slam the door in your face.

The second issue I see is not teaching time management and prioritization skills. These skills turn lead runners into investigators who can handle their cases from start to finish.

Is there a fear that the employee may learn how to handle their caseload? Is it the mindset that lower paid lead runners are easily replaceable parts in the machine, whereas skilled investigators will leave to go out on their own and compete with you? Why are you creating your drag? How can you boost yourself into orbit if you are carrying that mindset of resistance?

Edit reports with tracking in Word so the employee can see your editorial comments and learn from them. It might be faster at first to fix their mistakes, but you will always get stuck fixing their mistakes.

Performance appraisals done at the end of the year seem more like you are ambushing the employee so that you can justify a misery raise. What a demotivating exercise!

What if, on each and every case report, you gave them a reply that included measurement of:

T	Timeliness
S	Executing the investigative plan with substantive work in a logical manner
O	Meet or exceed the investigative objective.
B	Bonus points for getting the facts to justify an up-sell

They could agree or argue, based on their understanding of the unique circumstances that you may not be aware of right then and there, which is more helpful than defending a vague memory a year later.

What if the company bonus pool was tied into revenue growth and quality standards for each and every file handled by each and every employee?

What if the employee was given this data and asked to participate in their own performance appraisal? Hint- Honest employees are tougher on themselves than you would be. Those appraisal criteria are lifted right from their Position Contract:

- Results to be achieved (Expected outcomes and Performance Measures)
- Standards for this position (standards of Excellence)
- Work requirements for this position (Duties, Responsibilities, Accountabilities)

Bring your employees to conferences and seminars on the topics they are training in. Have them watch webinars and buy the guides or checklists they need for their work bag. Have them assist you in your training presentations. Allow them their time on the floor as the trainer.

How do you keep up their momentum of learning? That is your golden ticket.

"Enquiring minds want to know."

You can't train curiosity. You can only encourage it.

People ask me, "John, what are your proudest achievements in your career?"

I could talk about the cases that have appeared in the headlines or on TV. I could talk about the money I have made and the comforts that I have enjoyed.

Instead, this is what I tell them: "I am most proud of the investigators I have trained in my methods, and how they have blossomed in their own careers I have inspired aspiring investigators and hopefully passed on a legacy that will long outlive me and that they can pass on to further generations of investigators."

Do you want to be able to say that as well?

Will following hiring and training protocols also bring you closer to your financial goals?

SECTION SIX: HUDDLING

GIVE YOUR EMPLOYEES A STAKE IN THE OUTCOME

Be sure to stay to the end of this section. It holds the key to how to structure a buy-out.

The Milford, Connecticut Cracker Barrel had a beautiful round table in the back dining area reserved for the huddle.

Monday was an office day for International Missing Heir Finders, LLC, and a breakfast meeting started promptly at 8 am to kick off the week.

Only the occasional tour bus made it noisy, but otherwise, Dot, the usual server, was happy to greet them. Food was ordered and delivered. A light banter of the weekend's activity swirled about. The plates were cleared, and the meeting began.

Dot didn't mind. She was guaranteed to receive a 50% tip on the bill while she refilled coffee and hot water.

On that day, Claire led with a ten-minute presentation and handout on the latest Genealogical nugget she had unearthed. She is a Certified Genealogist and delighted in looking for obscure places to find the familial connections most important to the lifeblood of the company.

SECTION SIX: HUDDLING

Each employee would take turns sharing their latest discoveries.

The senior genealogist showed the assembled group the company's website which displayed reworked landing pages that helped heirs in their decisions to sign contracts with IMHF.

The executive assistant had worked with the Case Management company to figure out how to filter data by State and Tracer to show where they were getting quality cases for jacketing and the ponds where they were getting no bites. She and the marketing rep worked closely together.

A glass of water sat next to the table setting for the remote marketing rep who Skyped in. The marketer brought up the spreadsheet appearing on everyone's laptop, showing where tracers were being courted, added or dropped. Links to courts going online every day were also sent to the group.

The New York and New Jersey tracer, John regaled everyone with the latest Celebrity estate coming out of Manhattan. Like Los Angeles, it was the final resting place for many of the rich and famous. He often found good cases that hopefully the sharks had not gobbled up.

John, the owner, gave a recap on the highs and lows of courtroom battles on their cases from the previous week and which cases were on this week's docket.

He talked about the successes and failures in signing up heirs. The spreadsheet had every heir accounted for, and his batting average was there for everyone to see.

Where he found that heirs were contacted by other missing heir research firms that competitor data was on display as well, the group began to understand why they were guppies in some of the shark tanks around the country. Finding success around the country was proving more elusive than what was initially thought.

John ended with the financial numbers tallied from the previous week, compiled for him every Saturday by the bookkeeper.

Except for everyone's salary, all the company's numbers were available in the report. The critical numbers to the success of the company appeared in the cash flow snapshot. The health of the company was there for everybody to see and comment on.

Every number measuring everything the company did was transparent to every employee.

Did John just make this huddle stuff up? It was pretty radical.

Are you sharing all the numbers? Showing what was behind the magic curtain? Operations talking to Marketing, talking to Administration, talking about Legal, and employees talking directly to Ownership?

This is a model where everyone in a company from the janitor to the CEO has input in how to improve the company's performance and how that performance impacted on its financials, where everybody had a stake in the outcome.

Flashback to the previous September.

John A. Hoda and Jack Stack had a good laugh when they met for the first time over dinner and talked about how a missing heir research company and a dirty, greasy mid-western remanufacturing company of automobile and truck parks had so much in common.

When John toured the plant the next morning with others from around the country, he talked to a guy up to his elbows tearing down a diesel truck engine. The guy talked about how he was going to school at night to finish his degree in Business, how he sat on the factory's safety committee, and what his per hour labor charge-out would be if an engine was not worth remanufacturing and he spent too much time on diagnosing that issue.

SECTION SIX: HUDDLING

He showed precisely how is productivity affected the bottom line of the company. He had a higher degree of financial literacy and an understanding of the numbers than John.

John became a fanboy of Jack and went out to Springfield, MO, and St. Louis a couple of times as a practitioner in the Great Game of Business, GGOB for short–Open Book Management, to give it a generic name. Jack wrote both *The Great Game of Business* and *A Stake in the Outcome* with Bo Burlingham, then the editor of *Inc. Magazine*.

To borrow from the dust jacket of *A Stake in the Outcome*:

> "The pioneer of "open book management" Stack and twelve other managers began their journey in 1982 when they purchased their factory from its struggling parent company. Springfield Remanufacturing Company grew 15 percent a year while adding a thousand new jobs and the company's stock price rocketed from 10 cents a share to $81.60 per share in 2002 at the time of the book's publication." Bolded on the back flap: "In a successful ownership culture, every employee had to take the fate of the company as personally as an individual owner would."

Back to the Cracker Barrel.

The employees were well on track to become the eventual owners of the company. No equity had been apportioned yet. The company had not reached its mature state yet and was still growing.

This was the end goal that John had begun with when he started IMHF.

The date of transfer was not determined yet. When that day came:

Over three years, John would receive 50% of the company's revenue (25% in the first year, 15% in the second year, 10% in the third year).

The goal for the company was to have revenues of eight figures to the left of the decimal point. That was a brass ring worth reaching for.

The employees did not have to be saddled with a loan to buy the company and with long-term exposure to financial literacy and the methods of sharing best practices, were better positioned to remain successful. When the time came, they would continue to be practitioners in the Great Game of Business.

I see the biggest hurdle to get over is opening the books. You can no longer use the company's checkbook as your personal piggy bank. What you take out of the business weekly or monthly should be commensurate with the risk you took, your capitalization, the value of your original ideas, and your sweat.

Of course, you don't share how much Sally makes with Harry or what Harry makes with Larry. It's also little harder to justify your new Mercedes that year when you just canceled the company bonus plan.

Change has to start at the top and how you treat the people most responsible for mining the gold becomes glaringly apparent when you open the books.

Getting your people to engage their minds, not only in their job function but also in how they can continuously improve their processes is part of the fun. Watching them keep a sharper pencil on the line items reduces waste and unnecessary cost.

A team approach to growing the business takes a lot of the burden from your shoulders. It is harder to stop a team than just one player.

Hint: You are not the only one with great ideas.

If part of your "Boost" plan includes full-time employees, you owe it to yourself to read either book. I found *The Great Game of Business* to be as inspirational as it was informative.

SECTION SIX: HUDDLING

If hiring employees is new to you, I definitely recommend it to you. You have a blank slate to work with. Why not follow a game plan tested a thousand times over?

If opening the books scares you off, the huddle can still work with all the other measurables of your business without bringing up financials. The good folks at GGOB have other publications and workbooks that can assist you to build a business around your greatest assets."

GIVE YOUR EMPLOYEES A STAKE IN THE OUTCOME

SECTION SEVEN: SHARPENING THE SAW

WHAT GOT YOU HERE, WON'T GET YOU THERE.

Sad, but true. If you are coming at your business from a technician's viewpoint, the business of your craft has to be learned. If you are the refugee of a corporate or large organization with management skills, you still have to learn marketing. If you have marketing skills, you still have to learn strategic planning. What got you launched will not get you into orbit. You need to learn new skills. Most Private Investigation companies peak at the level of the owner's core set of competencies.

Action Coaching Business Coach

In 2004, John began attending a morning leads group with his local chamber of commerce. One morning, an Action Coaching Business Coach gave a short presentation on the math behind growing profits. At the end of the session, which was very informative, he mentioned he had a 12-week "boot camp" group class that would meet every other Wednesday for the Summer. John joined the class. It was an eclectic bunch. One attendee was looking to launch an Internet business, where he would match up clients with master mechanics who could give them a second opinion for a set fee on whether or not they needed a costly repair. There was a pest control company owner, a Landlord lawyer looking to become THE LANDLORD LAWYER in CT, an HVAC guy looking to boost his small company into Orbit (which he did). John couldn't remember what the last group member did, only that he always had excuses why the training wouldn't work with his business. He also never did his homework. Yes, there was homework. John was being taught about business in the practical sense, and the teachings were just as applicable to each member of the group.

John repeated the Action Coaching course at no additional charge when the course was revamped a year later, at the time he was about to launch IMHF. Both courses formed the basis for his financial literacy and some foundational training in how to approach and execute marketing campaigns.

When combined with the reading and training with the *Great Game of Business* (GGOB), John moved from having a team-based and project-based management strength to a more strategic view. He was prepared to market his new missing heir research firm and to teach his staff that their productivity had a direct impact on the company's financials.

His growth as an owner came at a time when he still attended conferences in Genealogy, both as a student and an exhibitor. The investment in learning what he needed to know paid off as he was able to ramp up IMHF to have a National footprint.

Pick Four and Mastermind Group

A fellow attendee of Tony's Chamber of Commerce leads group suggested forming a Pick Four Group.

This was the brainchild of Marketing Guru Seth Godin, who unabashedly gushes about being a disciple of the legendary Zig Ziglar.

Cassette tapes and workbooks from Zig's classes were the Holy Grail for marketers.

Godin distilled the **Pick Four** from Zig's teachings into a thirteen-week workbook where the user planned and executed four goals a quarter, hence the name Pick Four. The group members would meet for an hour after every other Tuesday's meeting to discuss in their allotted 15 minutes, what they had done on each goal in the past two weeks and what they planned to do in the next two weeks.

Weak goals or excuses were exposed pretty quickly, and suggestions on how to overcome the blocks or obstacles were suggested.

Tony was happy to receive the advice. Three decades of detective work didn't prepare him for all the facets of running a business. He was able to offer suggestions as it related to training and supervising from all those years of overseeing a detective squad in Mid-town Manhattan.

The group ran for a year, and at the end, they looked at what they had accomplished. Paying attention to goals on a daily, weekly, and bi-monthly basis allowed them to distill large goals into manageable tasks.

Tony found his next level to be a Mastermind Group. These

business owners came from different sectors of the economy, but all had an interest in Marketing. They met in person on the third Saturday of each month and rotated to each member's office. Tony was able to use Abe's conference room for the day that it was his turn. They all had uploaded their presentation materials in Google docs, and everyone had a screaming fast internet connection that allowed for real-time collaboration.

Each member had to give an hour-long presentation broken up into three 20-minute segments that allowed for feedback from the others. The first session was on what was working well, the second was on what was not, and the third was something new such as an app or Podcast or free e-book that could be shared with a group.

Tony held his own with these other heavyweight business owners. Who didn't want to hear from a former NYPD detective sergeant who was growing a PI business?

Hearing what worked with five other group members was great, but the learning hit home with the lessons from what wasn't working. The feedback was brutally honest and not much different from the autopsies on his squad's cases that resulted in acquittals or the DA refusing to sign an arrest warrant.

Tony couldn't keep up with all the actionable tips each member brought to the group. This executive-level mindset helped him get out of seeing everything through the eyes of a hard-boiled detective.

He was not on the street as much but was spending more time marketing and growing his business. Joe was working out great under Tony's tutoring.

Tony saw how college interns were a great source of quality hires with the other mastermind members. It wouldn't be long before they started taking work in the City, except for Staten Island, with their own interns who would be graduating soon from John Jay

College. The internships acted like a mini-probation period. The successful interns would be offered full-time jobs upon graduation.

Sub-contractors continued to supply part-time over-flow with two new full-time hires on the business Investigations side of Russo & Associates. Tony's skills as a supervisor were paying off, and he still worked the occasional case alongside his new people.

All of this growth was made possible by working his action steps from his Pick Four goals and then by aligning with the Mastermind Group.

APPSUMO- Thrive- Hubspot

Beth is excited about the design for her new company, Clark Intelligence Services.

She is vetting former military and civilian contractor intelligence professionals. She is using Basecamp to keep all the data under one cloud-based platform.

Her team is 100% remote. They use 24 Sessions to talk and show off their new toys. These platforms are integrated with Hubspot, their CRM.

Her new Administrative Assistant comes from Big Pharma and acts as their librarian. Tracey takes care of vetting all the tools and is continuously growing the drop-down menus for each remote employee and sweats the details of connecting all the platforms through another app named Zapier.

Her continuing education was propelled by her friendship with the APPSUMO people in Austin, Texas. They provided Beth with a first peek at some of their deals. APPSUMO is a leader in proving lifetime access to apps for online businesses, but they have been growing their learning-based products to teach customer skills such as project management and hiring practices. Their greatest strength for the licensed private investigation company is their suite of e-mail list building tools.

The CIS, LLC WordPress website is running on Thrive Themes, and Beth is a subscriber to Thrive University which has become her one-stop resource for all her online business training. They have a lean no-BS approach to explaining why some content converts and some don't. The video training is short, well-produced and speaks directly to growing revenues. They speak to regular business folks without falling back on language only techies can understand.

Hubspot has created a best practices library of resources related to Inbound Marketing.

After her morning workout routine, Beth spends the first 75 minutes of each working day with her online training modules, webinars, and classes, then take a short aerobic break while her favorite coffee brews, before opening her dashboard at precisely 9 am Central. She often muses to herself. You can take the girl out of the army, but not the army out of the girl.

SUMMARY

> What got you to where you are, won't get you to where you need to be.

Orbiting requires a boost, and that boost requires surrounding yourself with like-minded business people, using the tools of whatever method you choose to grow your skill sets. Give yourself permission to spend time on self-improvement.

Most PIs stop at the edge of their comfort level and retreat each time they get burnt. Making X and wanting to make 2 or 3X every working day is many times thwarted by risk aversion.

"Everything is okay. I don't want to take a chance on growth."

This translates into, "I am comfortable with the discomfort I feel now and am afraid of growing pains."

Part of that fear of failure comes from fear of the unknown.

Using a Business Coach or getting yourself into a Pick Four or Mastermind Group gives you access to people who have walked your path and have cleared out the thorns and snakes.

Companies that supply you with free or almost-free content do so to entice you to use their products or services, but the advice can be precisely what you need as you overcome drag and resistance.

SECTION EIGHT: BOOSTER ROCKET ENGINE, ENGAGE!

THE RESULTS

After payroll and overhead, Tony is making $1,000 every working day. He has a part-time admin that does much of the bookkeeping.

Tony signs off on payroll electronically and writes out most of the accounts payable checks.

Each employee has a company credit card with a $500 limit for gas, police reports, and court documents.

Joe and two full-time Criminal Defense Investigators (once interns) work along with two more investigators that handle Tony's original business plan, working with Business attorneys and CPAs in Eastern Long Island, which includes home-town Queens.

SECTION EIGHT: BOOSTER ROCKET ENGINE, ENGAGE

The two original subcontractors still help Tony with overflow. His profit margin hovers around 50%. He is down to working four days a week.

The time is evenly split between marketing, ride-alongs, and ownership. He has embraced the open-book management mantra and starts the week with a Monday morning huddle, much to the chagrin of the sub-contractors, who join in for the camaraderie and the free breakfast.

Joe is marketing to the Criminal Defense lawyers in their neck of the woods, while Tony continues to be the face of the company for Business clients. They grossed over a half million last year with a 10% increase projected for this year.

Tony rolled out a bonus plan tied to quality goals for each employee and net revenues. They already had a first-quarter "Bucket" pay-out, and everybody was pretty happy.

Then Tony's wife was diagnosed with breast cancer. They were able to treat it non-invasively, but it gave them both pause.

What were they working towards now? She was already pension-eligible from her Board of Ed job.

It was decided that by year's end, Tony would sell the business to his employees following a regular buyout plan. Joe would become the face of the company, and a significant rebrand was in the offing.

The Russos would travel and spend more time with their kids and grandchildren. The first payment would eliminate all of their real estate and car debt. The following years' payments would prop up an even healthier retirement nest egg. They could wait until the full retirement age for Social Security.

What started as a way to buff up his NYPD pension turned into a company he could sell to his employees.

Tony wouldn't miss the street. He had put his time in over the years between NYPD and Russo & Associates. He was pleased that he grew into a business person and was able to train his employees in his methods.

What started as a paying hobby ended up allowing him financial freedom from having to work with an excellent kicker at the end.

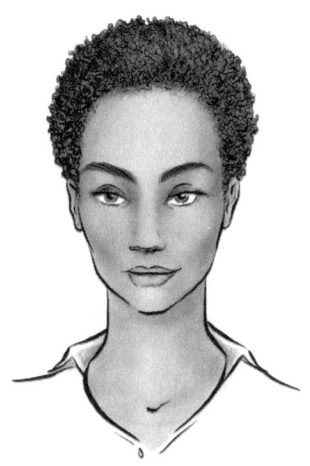

"I can live here," Beth thinks. She is resting on the beach of Phuket in Thailand after surfing Monsoon fueled waves for most of the morning. The water is blue she has never seen before. She had finished her fall and winter marketing at the major conferences with a booth for Clark Intelligence Solutions. She is supplying OSINT (Open Source Intelligence) to major corporations, large law firms, and businesses willing to pay her fees for in-depth reports that gave them actionable answers.

She sees that 3/4 of her business came from outside of Austin, Texas, and a healthy 10% of that work was international. After only two years of business in the B2B world, she has a full-time marketing team qualifying prospects at a dizzying pace.

The conferences also allow her to meet intell pros from all over the world. She has a way of convincing them to work with her. Maybe it has to do with a cutting-edge remote set up, surrounding them with the best tools to work with, and supplying them with a mission-critical sense of camaraderie.

She took a massive leap of faith at the beginning of the year to change from an LLC to a corporation, an employee-run company where she is the majority stockholder.

SECTION EIGHT: BOOSTER ROCKET ENGINE, ENGAGE

The lawyers and accountants were skeptical at first, but once it became employee owned and they saw the company's explosive growth the suits are now her most prominent evangelists. Everybody is thinking like an owner, and they have the tiger by the tail.

Her huddle is held online at midday to accommodate her employees in all four US time zones. They all laughed at her sleepy midnight demeanor from the night before, but she is amazed to see how well things work when they make decisions without running them by her first.

They are tough on each other in a good-natured way, when they add their critical numbers to the huddle board for Tracey to tabulate.

Beth's return flight is scheduled in two days, but a bunch of expats is heading down to the barrier reef in Australia for a snorkeling excursion. She hitches a ride with them. She will look at the dashboard after lunch.

What started as soft-launch to jettison herself from an Armored Guard service job into the B2C work of infidelity surveillances brought her to this dream life. She had a plan and no resistance to learning how to market and run it using best practices and taking full advantage of the Internet. She didn't stop there and took advantage of a growth opportunity which began as a weekend hobby, now turned into a gold mine.

THE RESULTS

Unfortunately, John had to close down International Missing Heir Finders, LLC. His youngest employee, who was listening politely during the huddles was now telling him the truth that John had been avoiding.

"You have to walk away while you still have some money on the table." The New York and New Jersey tracer said. "If you keep playing hands with this deck stacked against you, you will have nothing left."

He and John were stuck in bumper to bumper traffic coming back to Milford, Connecticut after racing to each surrogate court in four New York boroughs before closing time.

That afternoon, John had gotten bad news on two estates that were supposed to pay out that week. One became delayed when the judge gave yet another extension to the false heirs in the case to force IMHF to produce more evidence.

"This is how the good 'ole boys do it in Tennessee," John fumed to his lawyer.

The other case was worse. At the last minute, a federal tax lien was placed on the estate.

It seemed the decedent, an accountant herself, had not filed federal taxes for many years and the bulk of the estate would be eaten up by the lien. $175,000 net after the lawyer just evaporated, and they still had to pay him his 20K.

"You know what you are saying," John replied to his tracer.

"Yep."

SECTION EIGHT: BOOSTER ROCKET ENGINE, ENGAGE

They rode in silence for nearly twenty minutes before the tracer finally added, "We will survive, you have to think about yourself instead of finding a way to keep us working. If you said that you were going to keep trying to play, I'd say you were a gambling addict."

"You know I will have to lay you off," John said.

No employer likes to say those words ever, let alone a father to a son. It took much courage for John's son to deliver the bad news, but John had his listening ears on.

John had worked with a business coach from the Great Game of Business to create a dashboard for all the cases in the pipeline. The numbers were hard to tease out, but by going back to the beginning, they were able to create a living breathing document that told them some things in specific terms, and other things they could make reasonable assumptions on.

John no longer had competitive advantage in Connecticut, that much was for sure. The internet opened the doors where before they had to dig the files out of each probate court.

Searching for other jurisdictions around the country, where they could compete fairly against the entrenched missing heir competitors, proved difficult.

Most of the major metro areas, where the people with money resided, were shark tanks and IMHF were the guppies.

I have mentioned this phrase several times. I want to be fuzzy on purpose. I will not disparage a competitor's tactics without proof beyond a reasonable doubt. Yes, I am using a degree of evidence used in criminal cases.

As more courts went online, cases were made available to anybody with Internet access.

The market was flooded by competitors racing to the bottom

with lower and lower sign-up percentages. IMHF's thirty percent sign-up could not compete against others asking for nine percent.

John had been courted by a TV production company who filmed him in action finding and signing heirs. The "sizzle reel" failed to attract any Reality TV network. The instant fame and celebrity could not be mined for marketing gold.

In Connecticut, the cases closed in 11 months, from the time John found and signed heirs. The average time around the country was 22 months. The amount of money in the estate remained stable or increased before the final accounting was distributed.

Around the country, the original amount of the estate was drained by as much as 40% by the time all the payouts took place. Legal costs were triple for out of state attorneys.

The dashboard showed the numbers. The volatility of the market with its high-highs and low-lows could be assessed, and the assessment was not promising. That these two cases went bad were not entirely unexpected, but hastened the cash drain.

John met with each employee individually in the days leading to the next huddle at the Cracker Barrel.

At the huddle, John's eldest employee spoke up and said, "We could see the numbers as clearly as you. We were surprised that you didn't pull the plug sooner. We appreciate that you kept trying to find ways to keep it going. We all decided that we would keep doing our best until it was time to stop."

In the end, there was no finger-pointing or acrimony, and in December of 2011, International Missing Heir Finders held its last Holiday Party. It a meteoric rise and fall, for sure.

The unproven assumption that the early successes could be replicated around the country should have been proved (proof of concept) before making a significant investment of time, money, and personnel. IMHF could not break out of the atmosphere because of the drag of the external forces of the market and fell back to earth.

John would not be brutally honest with you if he told you that the lure of making a boatload of money was not a factor in going national.

Laying a six-figure check on the dinner table for the family to see, made payable to the company, was his way of validating to himself. To them, he was using his brains to the best of his ability. He thought he found a way to make the most money for his work-time.

Part of it was the timing of being at the right place at the right time with a curiosity of how to harvest the cases faster than his competitors.

Part of it was the drive to create a company he could sell to his employees, which had been his original goal with Independent Special Investigations, LLC.

Part of it came from a need to retire early and do something else in his second career, What AARP called an "Encore Career."

Did he not slow down at caution signals? Did he cruise through a few stop signs while humming a jaunty tune? Yes, he did, and yes, he was handed another character-building experience.

Endings Are Beginnings

With the money left on the table from IMHF, I was able to launch Elm City Detectives with the idea that I would turn off the lights and shut the door behind me when I was ready to ride off into the sunset for that encore career. I was working for Personal Injury Attorneys and Criminal Defense attorneys and began specializing in Exoneration cases. My son went to work with the soon-to-be owner of a Surveillance company in New York as his operations manager.

When that company was abruptly sold out from underneath them, and his position became redundant, we begin talking about forming Hoda Investigations, LLC, a P2P company serving Connecticut Trial Attorneys and Family Attorneys.

I work with my son, and we have a replicable and scalable marketing plan. We bill on the high end, even for the Northeast, and offer desirable flat rates to our clients. Our customers appreciate the value we bring to every case. I do my own bookkeeping and meet with my accountant quarterly to make sure that we are on target for our federal and state tax estimates.

We are proof that a solo with a part-timer or two most-timers can make the $1,000 every working day. It requires a full pipeline of cases lined up at least 10 working days out, and a replicable and scalable marketing plan that gets worked on at least 5 hours a week. Getting testimonials and referrals are our lifeblood, and we make sure to mark our territory at all the lawyer events.

I'm sitting in my favorite Starbucks on a Saturday afternoon as I finish this rough draft. My son, John, is doing much of the heavy lifting these days, but the old guy still goes out with the young gun every so often on a few select Innocence cases.

Our dashboard is a flip chart in the office where we measure how much we bill each week, how that compares with our goal and the variance. Besides an assignment log kept in Google Sheets, we show a color-coded stick count of how many and what type of cases we receive each week on the flip chart. We track the number of cold calls, contacts, appointments, and first-time customers. It's not crude, it's just not pretty, and it stares us in the face every working day. We do a cash flow snapshot twice a month. Cash is king. I haven't run out in 84 quarters, and I am not about to break that streak.

It has become a lifestyle business, one that my son will eventually take over. We are working on the succession plan. He has met

SECTION EIGHT: BOOSTER ROCKET ENGINE, ENGAGE

with and has worked for most of the customers. By the time this book is published, the website will be refreshed to really focus on the testimonials so crucial to a P2P company.

Twenty-one years ago, when I started my journey, I didn't know I would teach my son the business and pass on my skills and the company to him. Maybe there is a reason for everything.

Would I have liked to build ISI, or IMHF, to sell to my employees? The answer is yes, but I would never have learned the lessons that are so valuable to me and hopefully to you.

If I never ventured out of the insurance fraud investigation, I would never have learned about Criminal Defense or Forensic Genealogy. If everything went perfectly from the beginning, I would never have felt enough pain to change and grow.

CONCLUSION

Boosting your business to make $1,000 every working day is neither simple nor easy. The journey on your own path will begin at a different place, but some advice can apply to everyone along the way.

- Add planning time to your workday. Schedule it no differently than field appointments.
- Give, but don't abandon, some of your "job function" hats to other people to wear and automate as many repetitive functions as you can.
- Increase marketing time. Don't get lured into working cases all the time at the expense of growing your pipeline.
- The sooner you can share or shed the "fulfillment" portion of your time, the sooner you can start gaining altitude in your boost phase.
- Test and measure your marketing campaigns until you have a replicable and scalable method to attract your target audience. This can be as little as 5 hours a week and doesn't have to look like Mt. Everest to you. It is one step at a time, just like your boost plans.

SECTION EIGHT: BOOSTER ROCKET ENGINE, ENGAGE

- Fill your work pipeline out at least 7-10 working days. Plan the work and work the plan.
- Raise rates, create new offerings, and fire your worst customers.
- Be the go-to PI either for your territory or for your specialty.
- Refer cases to other PIs for a referral commission. Tout the services of your affiliates on your website.
- If you are not a world-renown expert or highly sought specialist, determine what you can do to upgrade your skill sets to be able to charge more for your time
- For most Private Investigations owners, going deeper into a market–and not wider–allows for better focus and immunity from competition.
- Track your progress. "That what gets measured, gets done," says Peter Drucker, Management Guru.
- Find a coach or others to help you elevate your game. This lowers the fear-based self-imposed obstacles in your path. Accountability is an essential component of your motivation.
- Build HR systems to recruit, hire, train, supervise, and appraise the people you need to boost your business into orbit. Using the checklists here are just the beginning.
- Creating a three-ring binder, literally or digitally, is an essential step if you plan to off-load any of your job functions to employees.
- "You gotta wanna." The good folks at the Great Game of Business coined this phrase.

Now, take out a clean sheet of paper, sit down with your favorite beverage, and get started.

"Ain't nothing to it, but to do it," an old homicide detective once told me.

CONCLUSION

To Jack Stack, Tim Ferriss, Noah Kagan, and Joanna Penn for challenging me to take my business to the next level

NEED MORE HELP?

If you are launching your business soon and have questions or you are having trouble getting your company off the ground, I am available for a FREE 30-minute consultation. Please go to the contact form at www.ThePICoach.com and schedule a phone call with me. It may be an easy fix.

Also

I only coach PIs and limit my time to just eight individual sessions a week so that I can concentrate on helping each client reach their goals and achieve a life/work balance.

ABOUT JOHN A. HODA, CLI, CFE

John A. Hoda is a licensed private investigator, blogger, and podcaster. He coaches other PIs how to be successful at **ThePICoach.com**

He graduated in 1975 with a B.S. in Criminology from Indiana University of Pennsylvania.

He is a former police officer, insurance fraud investigator, and has run several PI businesses over three decades.

He has written numerous articles for PI Magazine and is the creator of the DVD: *The Ultimate Guide to Taking Statements*. His cases have headlined in the Philadelphia Inquirer and the New Haven Register. He sat on the board of the National Association of Legal Investigators and the CT Assoc of Licensed Private Investigators. He is a Certified Legal Investigator and a Certified Fraud Examiner.

John also writes fiction and has been a lifetime athlete playing club soccer and playing/coaching semi-professional football.

His podcast audience at My Favorite Detective Stories is growing every day. John interviews past and present investigators about their specialties and teases out what it takes to make for a successful investigation. The entire podcast catalog can be found at **JohnHoda.com**

OTHER BOOKS BY JOHN A. HODA

Get your FREE *Mugshots: My Favorite Detective Stories* downloaded in your favorite format right to your inbox by going to **JohnHoda.com.**

Come ride around the country with veteran investigator John A. Hoda as he searches for the truth. He has selected great stories from a forty-plus year career and keeps serving them up like free refills at the all-night diner.

Non-Fiction

How to Launch Your Private Investigation Business: 90 days to Lift Off!

How to Market Your Private Investigation Business: Less Than 5 Hours a Week, Really!

How to Rocket Your Private Investigation Business: The Complete Series

Fiction

Odessa on the Delaware: Introducing Marsha O'Shea

A Crime Thriller with a mystery twist set in Philadelphia pitting a Russian mob enforcer against a homeless Marine Corp veteran. FBI Agent Marsha O'Shea is drawn into the case with a secret pushing her to follow the clues, only to uncover a greater secret that may get her killed in the final showdown.

Phantasy Baseball: It's About A Second Chance.

A thirty-nine-year-old little league coach discovers he has a magical pitch and gets a one in a million chance to try out for his beloved Philadelphia Phillies. He is unprepared for the roller-coaster magic-carpet ride in the Big Leagues.

ACKNOWLEDGMENTS

Rekka Jay for Cover Design, Illustrations, Editing, Formatting, Layout, Patience and Forgiveness.

My advanced copy readers who saved my butt countless times: Luis Reyes, Ron Getner, Rich Robertson, Brandon Perron, Cynthia Hetherington, Brian Ritucci, Jayne McElfresh, Lisa Garcia, Kate Minchin, Burt Hodge, Tony Raymond, Paul Rubin

The **Written Word-Milford Writers Group** for their support and encouragement.

Thanks to all.

www.ingramcontent.com/pod-product-compliance
Lightning Source LLC
Chambersburg PA
CBHW020110020526
44112CB00033B/1167